MiG PILOT SURVIVAL

★ ★ ★

RUSSIAN AIRCREW SURVIVAL EQUIPMENT AND INSTRUCTION

Alan R. Wise

Schiffer Military/Aviation History
Atglen, PA

ACKNOWLEDGEMENTS
I wish to thank the following people for assisting in the creation of this book:

Yuri Altshuler
Michael S. Breuninger
David Cherolis
Scott Ferguson, U.S. Air Force Museum
Jeff Greene, Green Otter Productions
Ted Lawson
George Peterson
Anton & Julie Savchenko
David Shablak
Ruth Shablak
Missy Sharp
David Smith
N. Scott Spurling

DISCLAIMER

All items depicted in this book are intended for collectors and display use only. Actual use of the items is not implied nor recommended. The information presented in this book is for historical benefit only. Wilderness survival training is a serious matter and should be instructed only by trained experts.

Book Design by Robert Biondi.

Library of Congress Catalog Number: 96-68819.

Printed in China.
ISBN: 0-7643-0130-6

We are interested in hearing from authors with book ideas on related topics.

Published by Schiffer Publishing Ltd.
77 Lower Valley Road
Atglen, PA 19310
Please write for a free catalog.
This book may be purchased from the publisher.
Please include $2.95 postage.
Try your bookstore first.

PREFACE

In March, 1965, after becoming the very first human to "walk in space," Cosmonaut Alexei Leonov, along with his crew mate Cosmonaut Pavel Belyayev, suffered the failure of their Voskhod 2 spacecraft's automatic re-entry computer. The resulting switch to manual allowed their safe return to earth, but over 1,200 miles off course! They landed in a remote snow-covered forest in the Ural Mountains. A rescue helicopter located the men within a few hours, but the terrain was too rugged and the sub-zero weather too poor to land anywhere within twelve miles of the site. Armed with only their survival kit and their training, Leonov and Belyayev made camp and spent an uncomfortable night alone, except for an occasional hungry wolf which Leonov reportedly fended off with their machete. The next day help arrived on foot with additional supplies, and after a second night in the snow, they hiked to safety, having spent double the time in the hostile wilderness of their homeland than of space. To have succeeded in completing an extremely dangerous space mission only to die of exposure in their own country was unthinkable. Yet it was entirely possible had it not been for their excellent training and equipment. To this day Russian survival training remains very extensive, and very serious.

The goal of aircrew survival training is to sustain the life of crewmen in any environment for a limited period of time, using all available resources, and to promote rescue by friendly forces. This involves intense instruction, carefully prepared manuals, and the use of materials gained from three sources: specific survival equipment, aircraft materials, and natural resources. Much information is available relating to U.S. aircrew survival such as issue manuals and "United States Combat Aircrew Survival Equipment" by Michael S. Breuninger (Schiffer Publishing Ltd.). However, information concerning other nations' capabilities is difficult to obtain. Russian survival technology is significant for the following reasons: Russia is the largest nation on earth having within its borders vast wilderness regions which are, likewise, the largest in the world and comprise a total area far greater than that of the entire United States, including Alaska.

Virtually every hostile environment known to the planet exists in Russia, from the long, sub-zero Siberian winter, to the 122 degrees F. of the southern deserts, to the humid, mosquito-infested forests of Sahkalin Island. Rugged mountain ranges, savage rivers, endless forests, tundra, and desert are matched with incredible distances between cities, villages, roads, etc. In addition to these natural dangers, some regions are inhabited by minority populations who are extremely hostile towards any outside military personnel. In short, Russia's back woods can be a pilot's worst nightmare.

It is therefore easy to appreciate that in peace time a Russian airman faces a greater chance of finding himself in a serious survival situation upon suffering the loss of an aircraft than perhaps any other airman in the world.

Recollections from other lost crews abound with legendary accounts of surviving under amazing circumstances. Fending off wolves, bears, and even Siberian Tigers with hand-made spears and fire are not uncommon. Treks across great distances in extreme weather conditions while assisting injured comrades are also recalled in numerous narratives.

Russia's history and culture have played a significant role in the development of their survival theory. The design and use of some gear – such as edged tools – follows traditional models which have been in use for hundreds of years. The particular lifesaving training and requirements of Russian aircrews has also resulted in some survival equipment so unique there is no foreign counterpart, while other items are ingeniously designed to meet the crewmen's specific needs.

All of these factors, combined with lessons learned during the bloody war in Afghanistan, has resulted in a fascinating and thoroughly developed strategy of assuring the survival of aircrews and cosmonauts. There are three basic segments which also define the three chapters of this book: Survival Equipment and Related Components, Aircrew Survival School Techniques, and the Survival Manual.

CONTENTS

INTRODUCTION

The equipment detailed in this book is entirely of former Soviet manufacture and issue. The equipment is exported and utilized by many other nations who fly Russian aircraft. Wherever possible, proper designation and nomenclature is listed. Materials, photographs, and information were obtained from a number of sources and therefore the extent of detail varies. No photographs were available of some items, while of other items, limited details were available. Every reasonable effort was made, however, to gain as much information as possible for this book.

The aircrew survival techniques information was obtained from first hand sources as well as information gained from military publications besides the manual reprinted in Chapter 3.

The manual is as much a direct translation of the Russian text as is practical. A word-for-word translation is not desirable due to differences in the structure of the two languages. Any translation is a compromise between intended meaning and proper grammar. In this, we remained flexible, leaving some grammatical errors to provide a "flavor" and to impart a sense of translation to the material. Many cultural aspects appear in the text as well as what must be attempts at humor: "If you eat the liver of a Polar Bear, here's what will happen to you . . . So, NEVER eat Polar Bear liver, even if you are very hungry!"

The illustrations and their numbers are from the original manual. Number 10-5909 is not translated as an example of the original.

CHAPTER 1

SURVIVAL EQUIPMENT AND RELATED COMPONENTS

Aircrew Survival Kits

In Russian, a survival kit is designated as a Portable Emergency Kit or by the abbreviation NAZ. The number or letter following the designation is relative to series of kit of a particular application. For example, the NAZ-3 used aboard the Soyuz spacecraft is the third model spacecraft kit and not a predecessor of the NAZ-7 used in ejection seat equipped aircraft.

NAZ-7

The NAZ-7 is a soft type seat kit primarily used in ejection seat equipped aircraft beginning with the MiG-23 and Su-17. It is used in all newer MiG aircraft, as well as in most current Sukhoi fighters. Several other military aircraft use the NAZ-7 as a strap-on parachute kit. The NAZ-7 is an extensive kit and has three compartments with the two smaller pockets designed for a variety of components to modify the kit for arctic, desert, or ocean conditions.

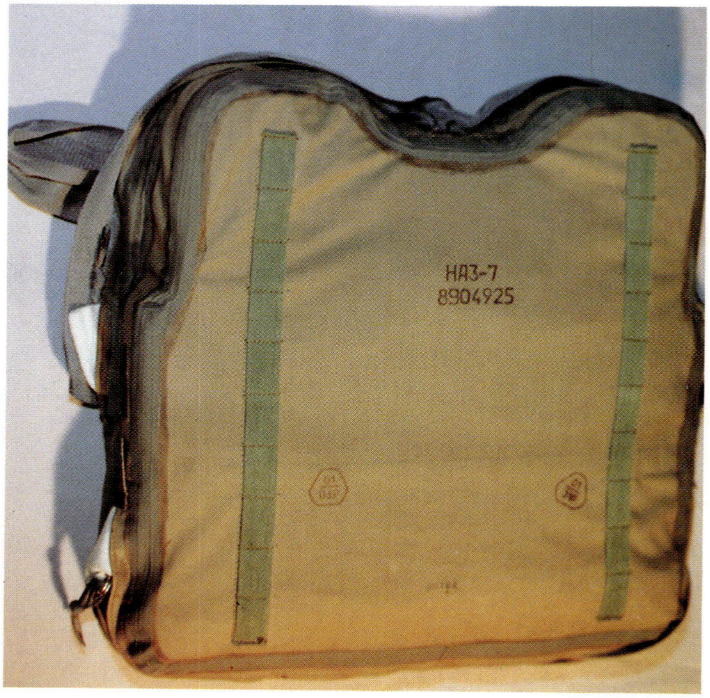

The NAZ-7 container carries an individual identification number clearly marked on top and registered to the particular aircraft.

The underside shows four straps which are used to attach the kit to any type parachute harness and also allows the kit to be carried as a backpack.

OPPOSITE BELOW: The components of the main compartment of the NAZ-7 are all secured by elastic straps to a foam-covered aluminum tray with a handle for easy removal. On the left are the survival manual and water bag sealed in plastic and orange antenna pouch. Every item is secured to the kit by nylon "dummy" cord and all containers are of aluminum.

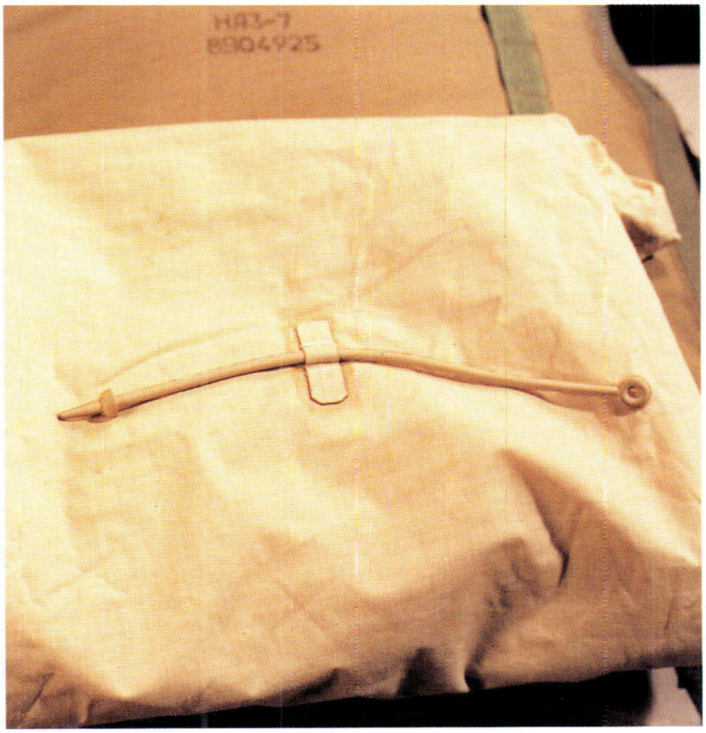

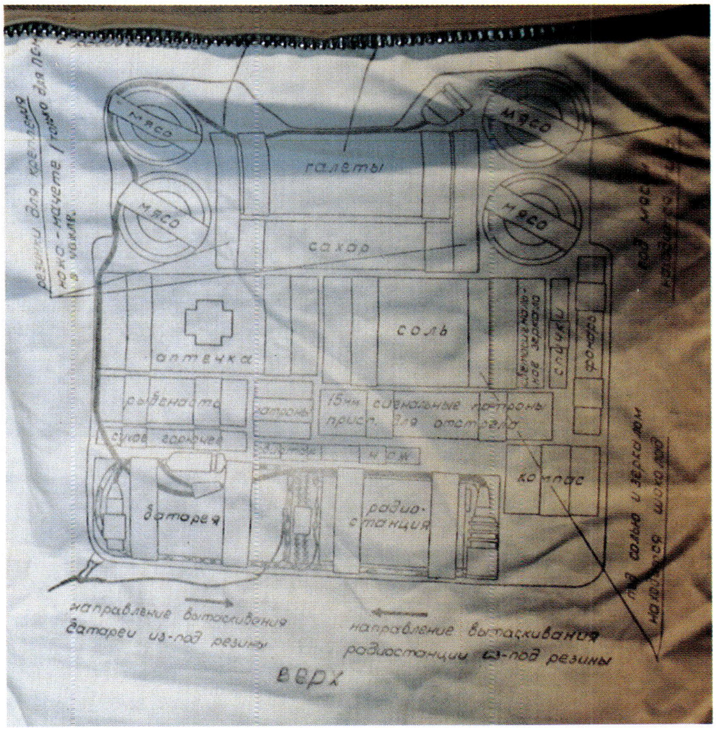

LEFT: The main compartment is made water tight by way of rubberized material and a heavy elastic band. In this manner, contents are protected and an empty kit container can be used as a water carrier or, filled with air, as a floatation device. RIGHT: A diagram of the main compartment components is printed on the rubberized clothe flap.

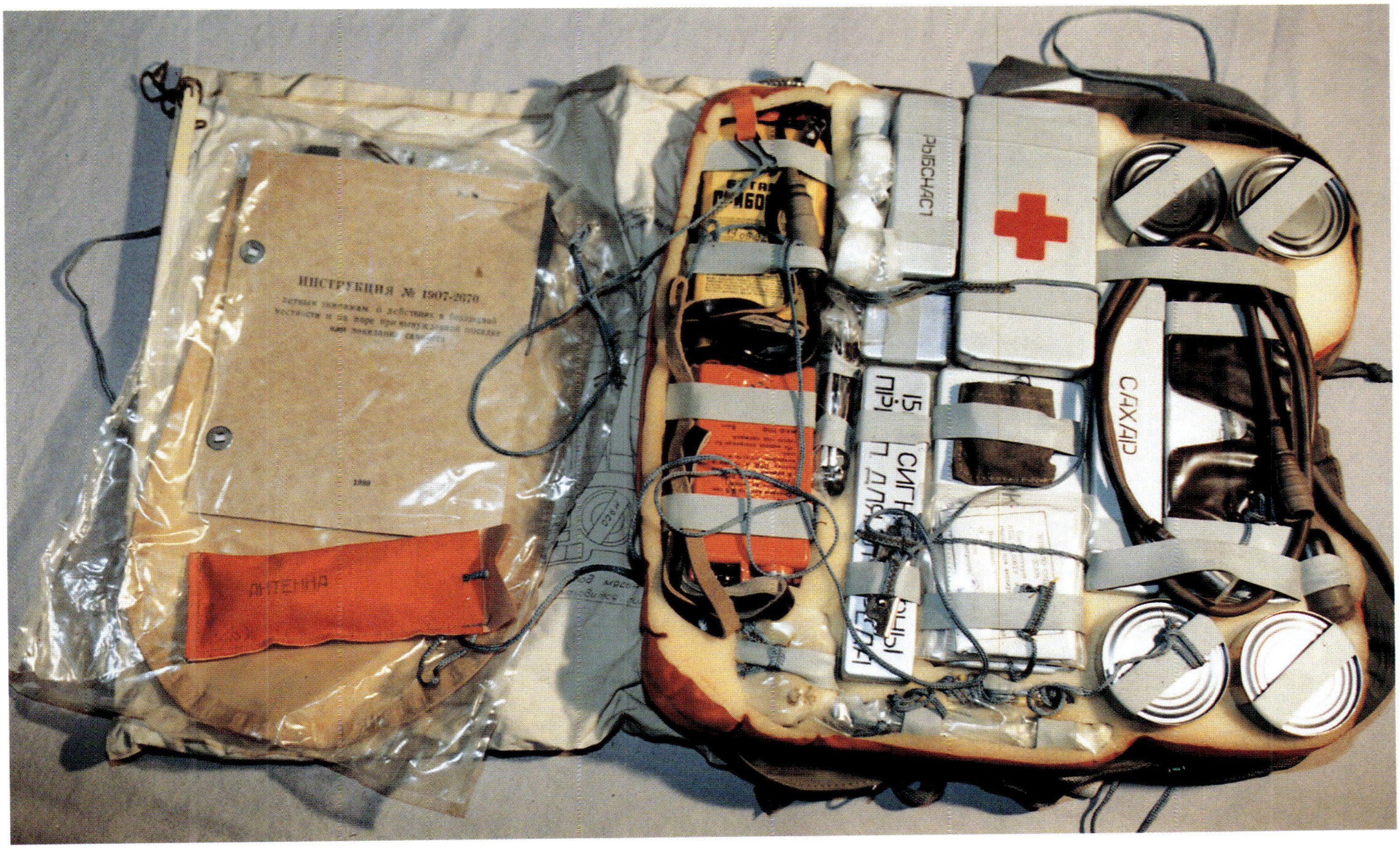

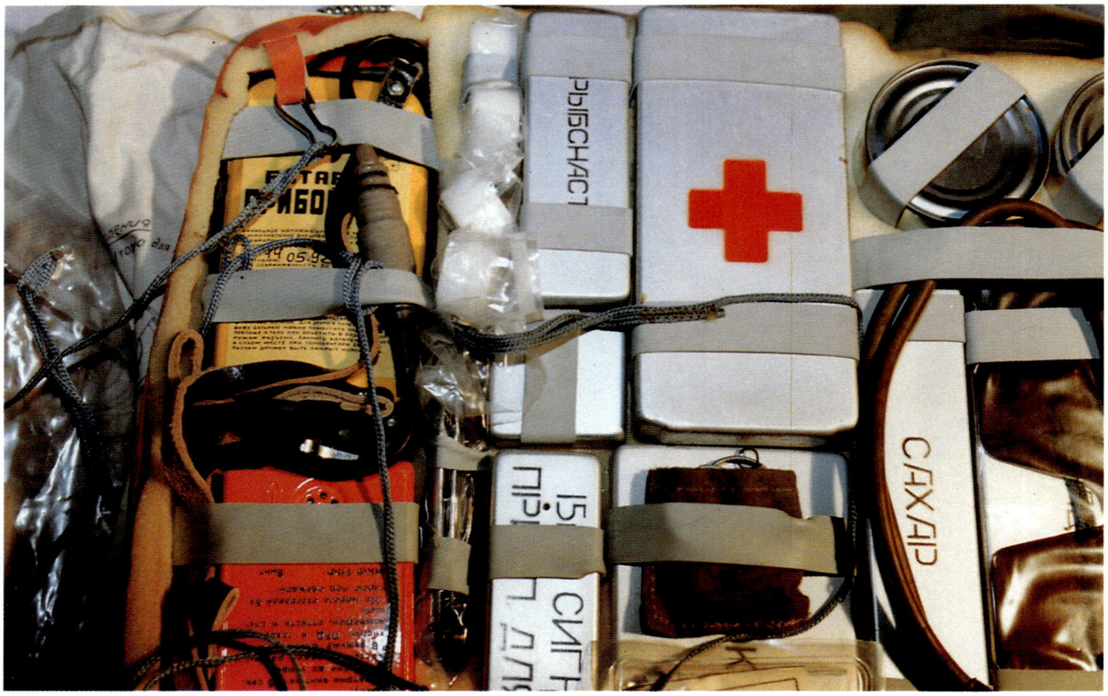

NAZ-7 components (left to right, in kit): "Priboy-2S" battery for radio; four fire starters made of granulated ethyl alcohol; fishing kit; medical kit (with red cross). Below fishing kit is ammunition box.

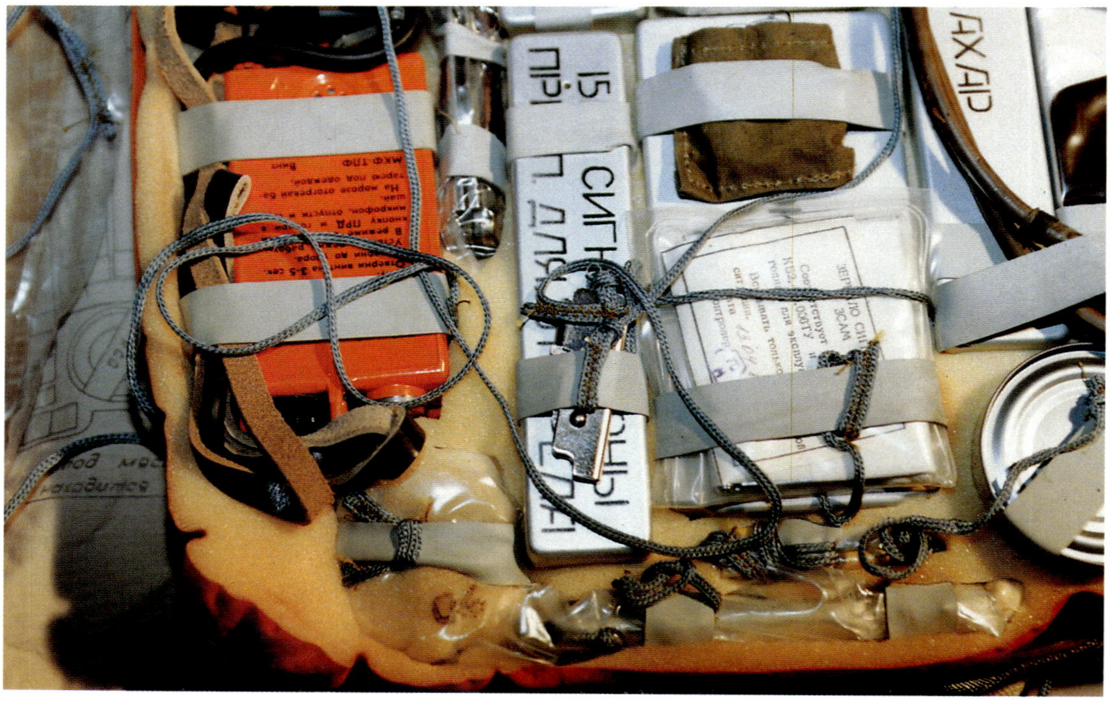

Left to right, in kit: Orange R-855-A1 radio with leather straps; folding lock-blade knife in plastic bag; container for 15mm signal flare set with folding can opener on top; container for chocolate bar with wire saw and signal mirror on top. Below, sealed in plastic and protective foam is the wrist compass; penlight; extra bulb; whistle; and nine waterproof matches with striker.

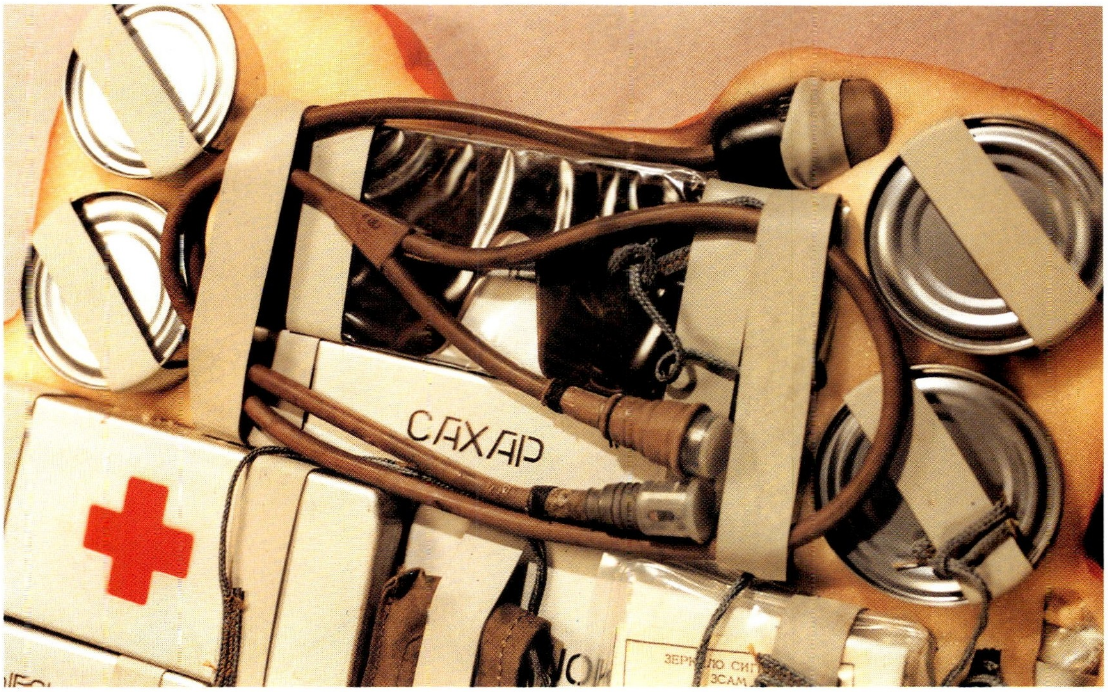

Center, in kit: Radio to helmet connecting cord; container for sugar cubes; sunglasses; container for survival biscuit (under sunglasses) and four round cans of fish such as tuna.

Detail of small items: (left to right): Plastic whistle has hard cork "pea"; wire saw with protective cover; folding bottle opener and can opener designed similar to famous U.S. Army P-38; aluminum penlight is waterproof and is switched on by turning ring 90 degrees. It uses two standard AA batteries.

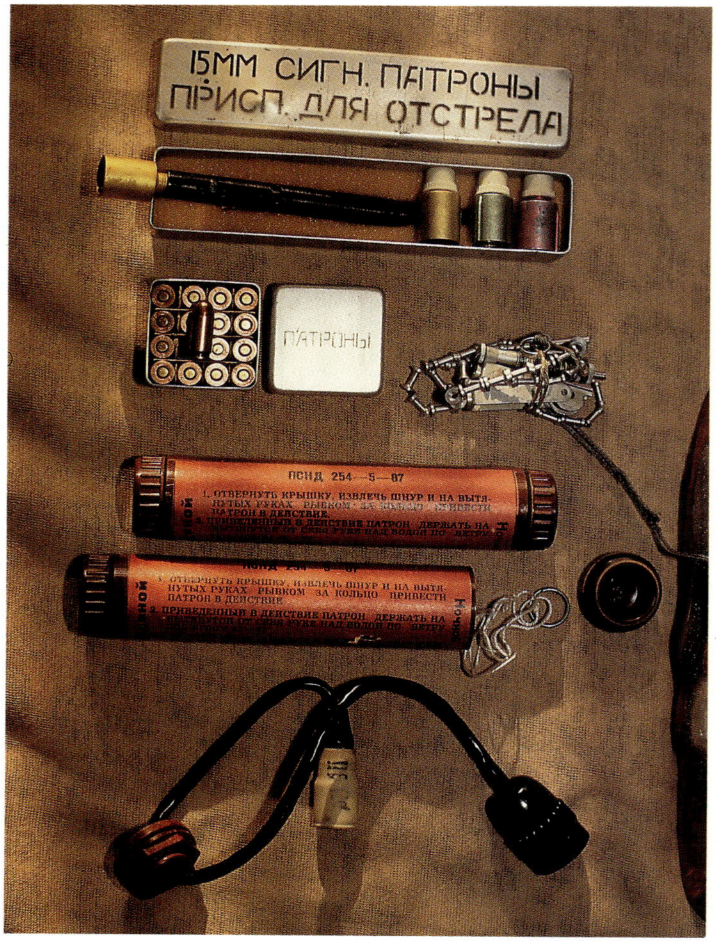

Top to bottom: 15mm flare kit showing launcher with color-coded yellow flare mounted and yellow, green and red flares in box. Ammunition box holds sixteen 9x18mm Makarov pistol cartridges and next to this is a jointed type radio antenna. Two PSND hand-held flares are often carried in NAZ-7 kit in ocean configuration. Removed end cap shows pull cord for activation. One end of PSND flare offers 30-second orange smoke for day use and the other is a bright red flare for night. Electrical connector adapts radio to communications helmet used by high-altitude pilots.

Left to right, top to bottom: High-energy white chocolate bar is wrapped in wax paper and divided into four parts. Jointed radio antenna is extended by applying tension to center guide wire with device at the base. Brown survival biscuit is wrapped in wax paper. Sixteen sugar cubes are also wrapped in wax paper. Canned meats can be from outside sources depending upon unit. In this case, the former Czechoslovakia.

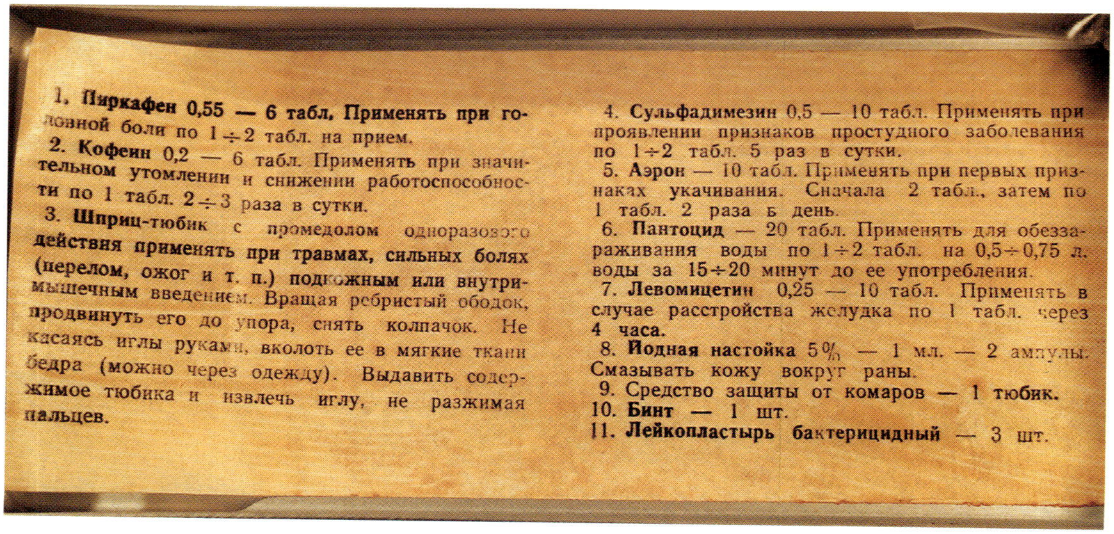

1. **Пиркафен 0,55 — 6 табл. Применять при головной боли** по 1÷2 табл. на прием.

2. **Кофеин** 0,2 — 6 табл. Применять при значительном утомлении и снижении работоспособности по 1 табл. 2÷3 раза в сутки.

3. **Шприц-тюбик** с промедолом одноразового **действия применять при травмах, сильных болях (перелом, ожог и т. п.) подкожным или внутримышечным** введением. Вращая ребристый ободок, продвинуть его до упора, снять колпачок. Не касаясь иглы руками, вколоть ее в мягкие ткани бедра (можно через одежду). Выдавить содержимое тюбика и извлечь иглу, не разжимая пальцев.

4. **Сульфадимезин** 0,5 — 10 табл. Применять при проявлении признаков простудного заболевания по 1÷2 табл. 5 раз в сутки.

5. **Аэрон** — 10 табл. Применять при первых признаках укачивания. Сначала 2 табл., затем по 1 табл. 2 раза в день.

6. **Пантоцид** — 20 табл. Применять для обеззараживания воды по 1÷2 табл. на 0,5÷0,75 л. воды за 15÷20 минут до ее употребления.

7. **Левомицетин** 0,25 — 10 табл. Применять в случае расстройства желудка по 1 табл. через 4 часа.

8. **Йодная настойка** 5% — 1 мл. — 2 ампулы. Смазывать кожу вокруг раны.

9. Средство защиты от комаров — 1 тюбик.

10. **Бинт** — 1 шт.

11. **Лейкопластырь бактерицидный** — 3 шт.

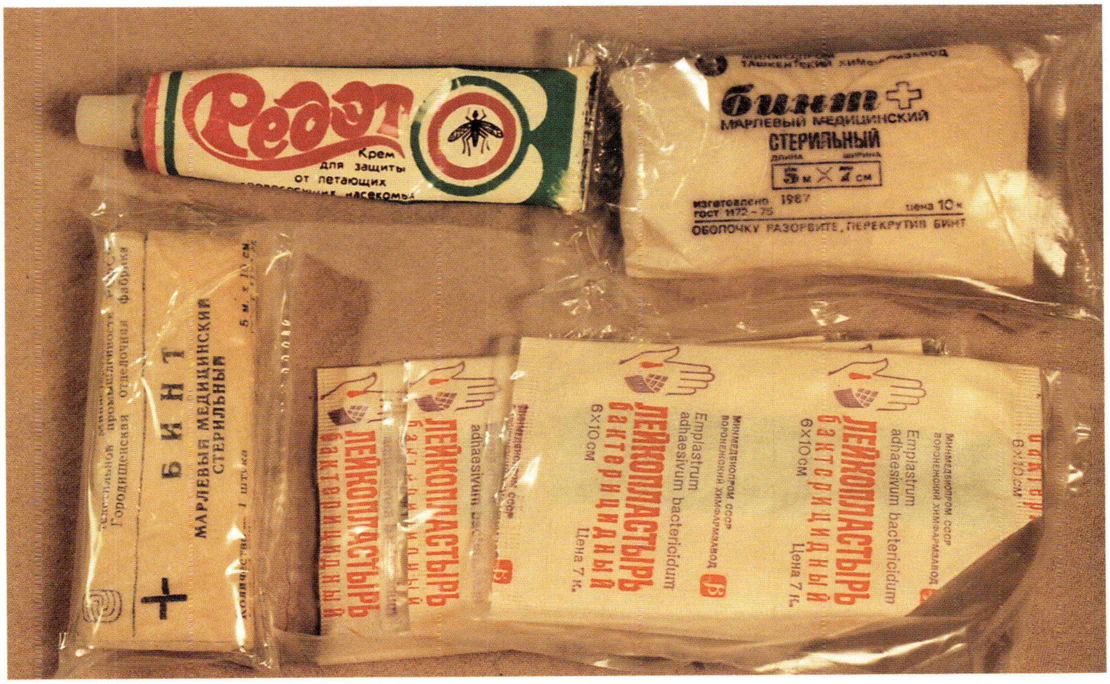

Left to right: Medical kit includes: Insect repellent cream; 5 meter x 7 cm. gauze roll; bandage; three 6x10 cm. adhesive bandages. Insect repellent instructions suggest: "a thick layer over all exposed skin areas, avoiding eyes and any cuts or abrasions. Wash off with water. Can be applied three times a day."

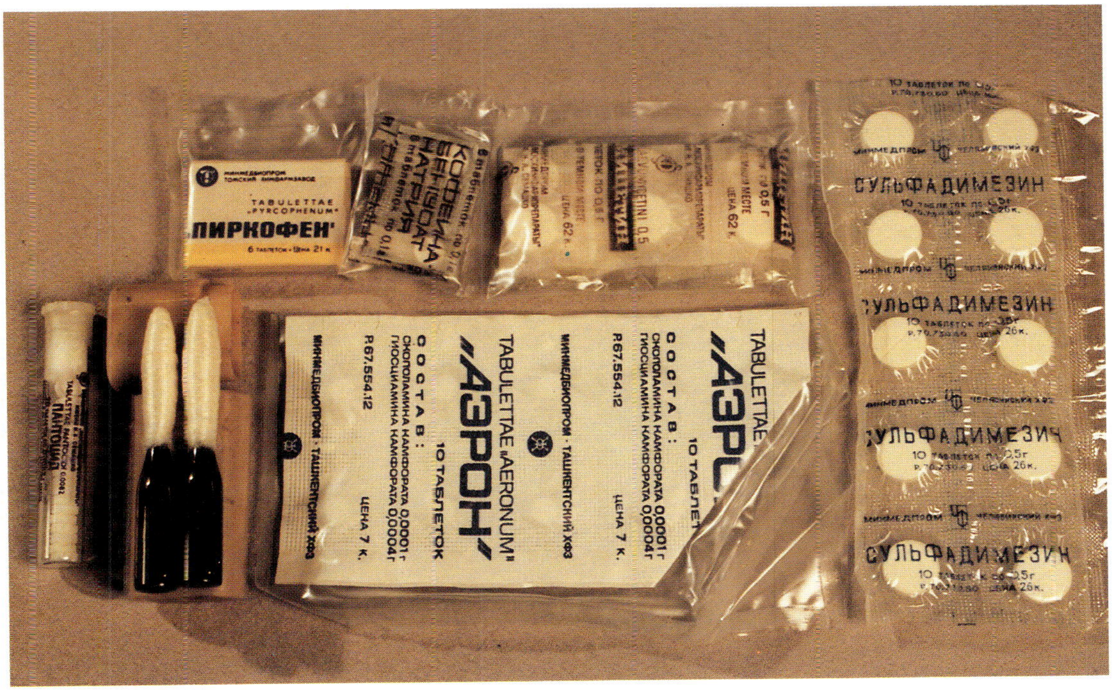

Left to right, top to bottom: 6 "Perkafene" awake pills, 6 caffeine pills, 10 Antibiotics, 10 Sulfide pills, 20 water purification tablets, two iodine ampules with protective case, 10 aspirin tablets.

OPPOSITE BELOW: The top of the medical kit lists its contents with instructions: **1**. "Perkafene" Commercial awake pills (6): 1-2 pills per dose; **2**. Caffeine pills (6): 1 pill 2-3 times a day; **3**. Morphine syrette (2): inject into major muscle for pain relief from major injury; **4**. Sulfide pills (10) 1-2 pills, 5 times per day; **5**. Aspirin (10) 1 pill twice a day; **6**. Water Purification pills (20): 1-2 tablets for each 0.5-0.75 liter, shake well, wait 15-20 minutes before use; **7**. Antibiotics (10) 1 pill every 4 hours; **8**. Iodine ampules (2) 5%, 1 ml. each; **9**. Mosquito repellent; **10**. Gauze bandage; **11**. Sterile adhesive bandage.

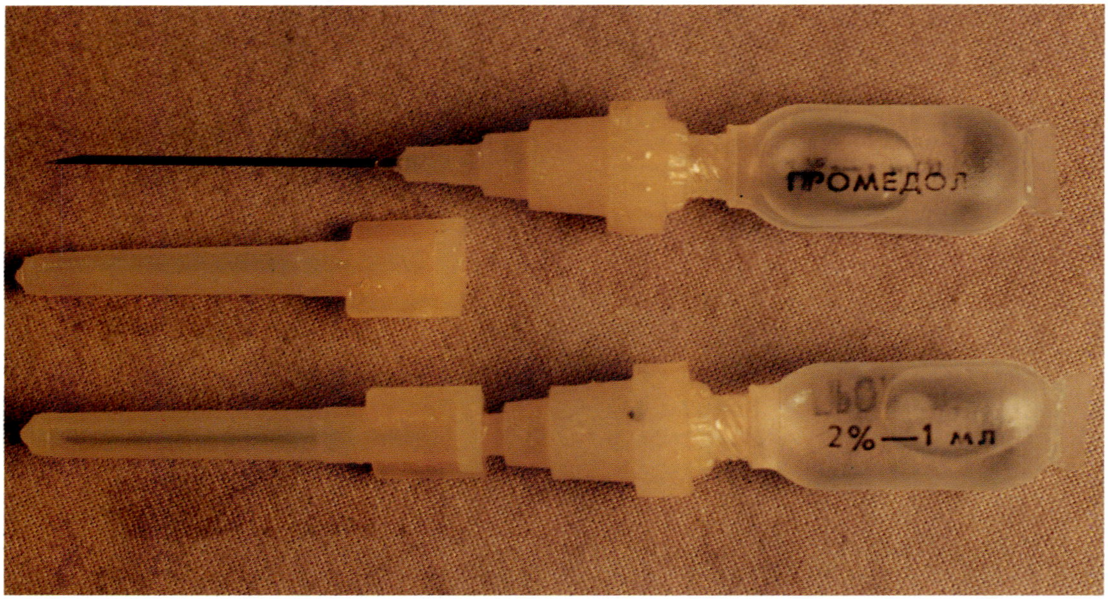

Pair of Morphine syrettes, 2%, 1 ml. solution.

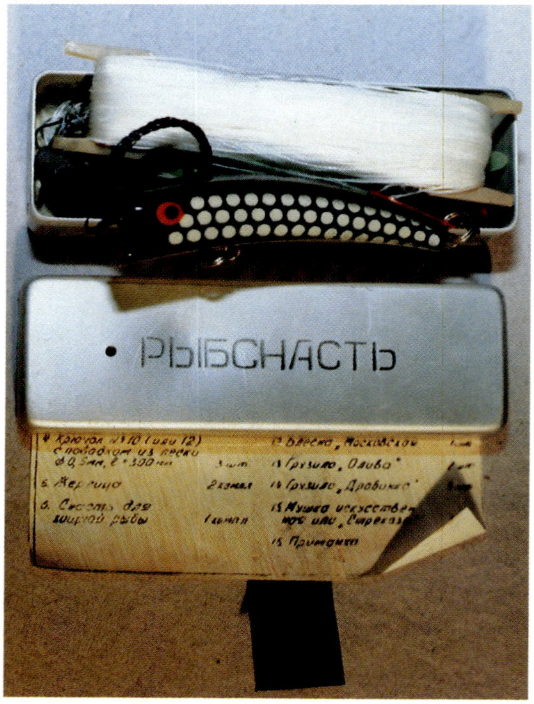

NAZ-7 fishing kit is also used in Soyuz NAZ-3.

Fishing kit includes a wide variety of tackle for a wide variety of fish. Brightly colored yellow and red clothe is for creating certain types of lures.

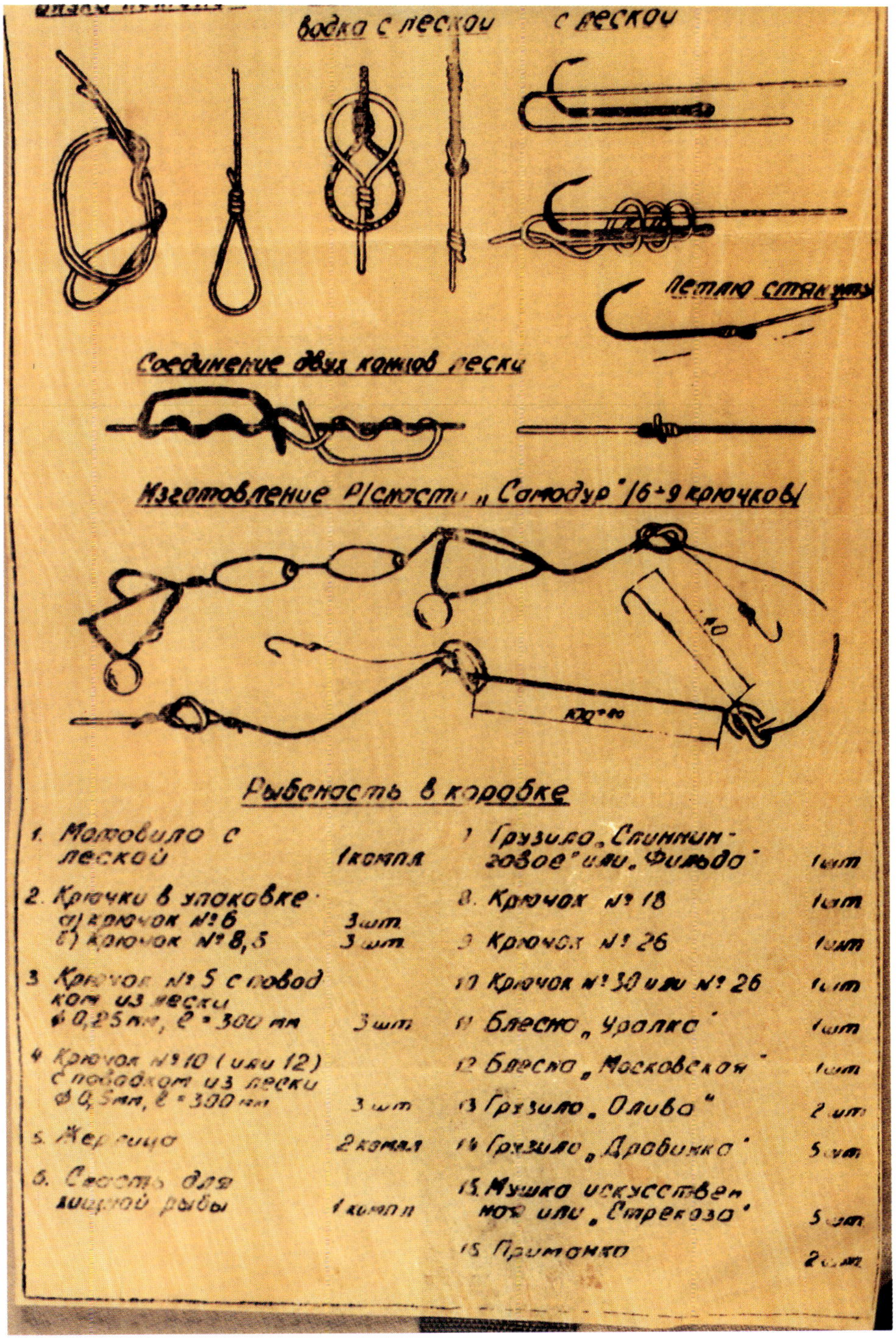

Fishing instrt.ctions are located in the top cover of kit.

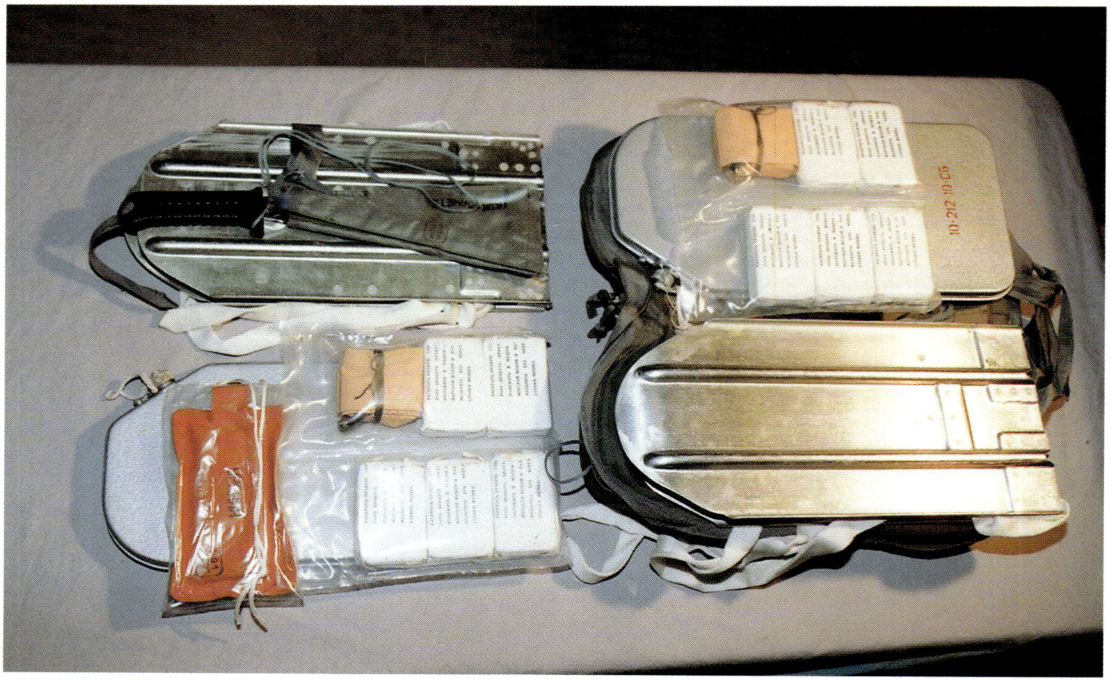

The two smaller compartments of the NAZ-7 adapt the kit for certain conditions: two 1.5 liter water containers for desert, one pair of folding snowshoes and machete for arctic, and two sets of desalting kits with five desalting packets and one bag each with one dye marker for ocean.

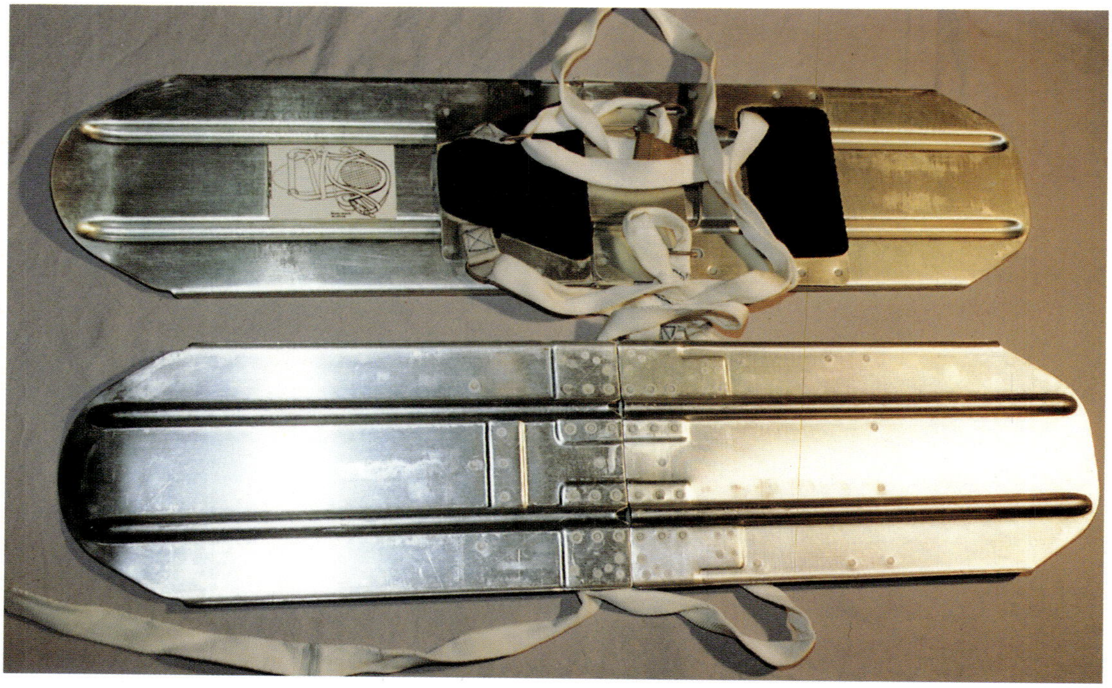

Folding snowshoes are made of aircraft grade aluminum.

Snowshoe is locked in open position by sliding cloth tab forward, pushing two lock pins into place.

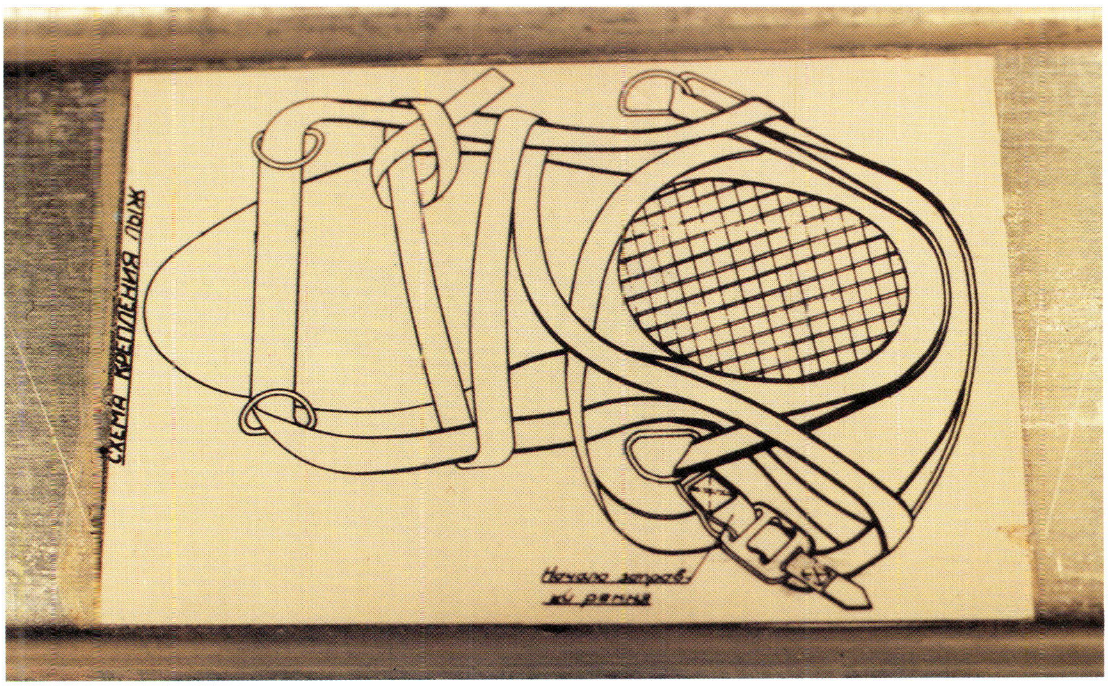

Universal mounting illustration appears very confusing.

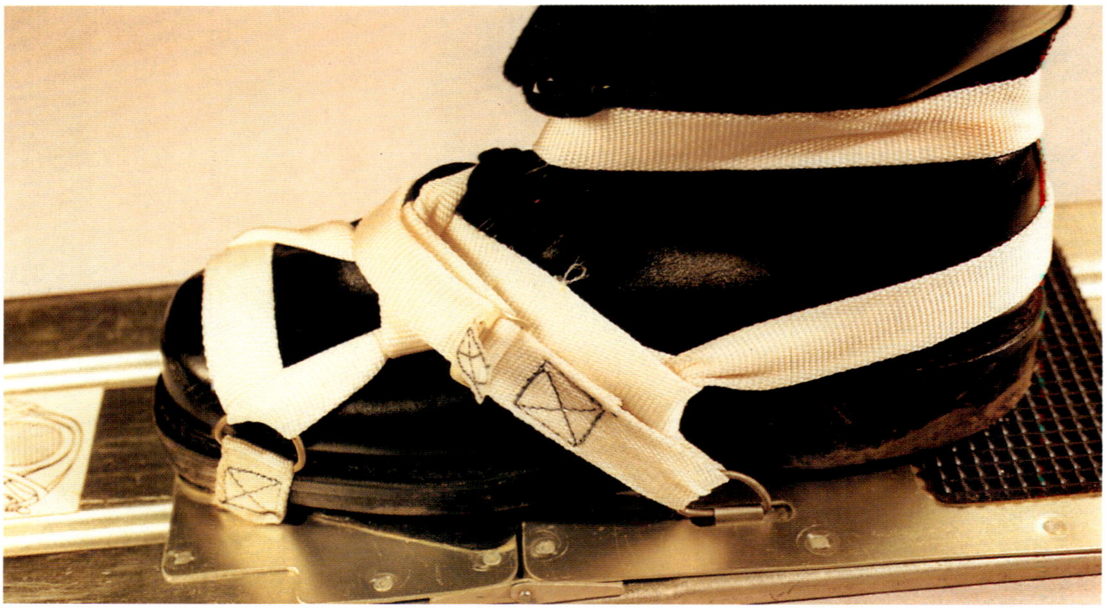

ABOVE: White nylon strap secures boot very well to snowshoe. BELOW: Lashing system is complex, but works.

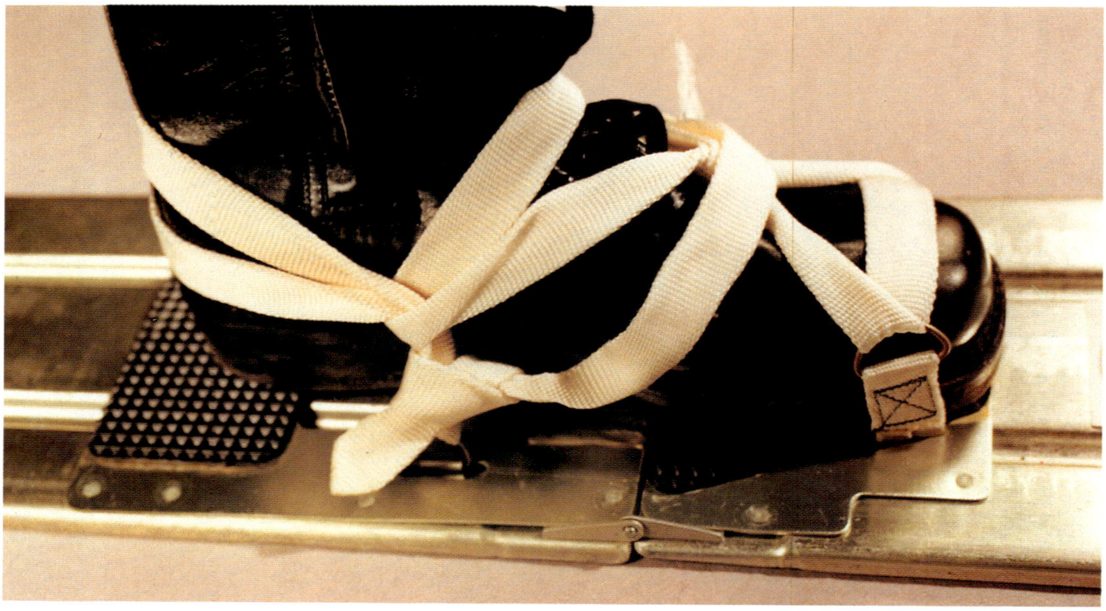

In actual use, snowshoes work very well.

Each desalting kit contains five packets and one filter bag. Shown with 1.5 liter water container.

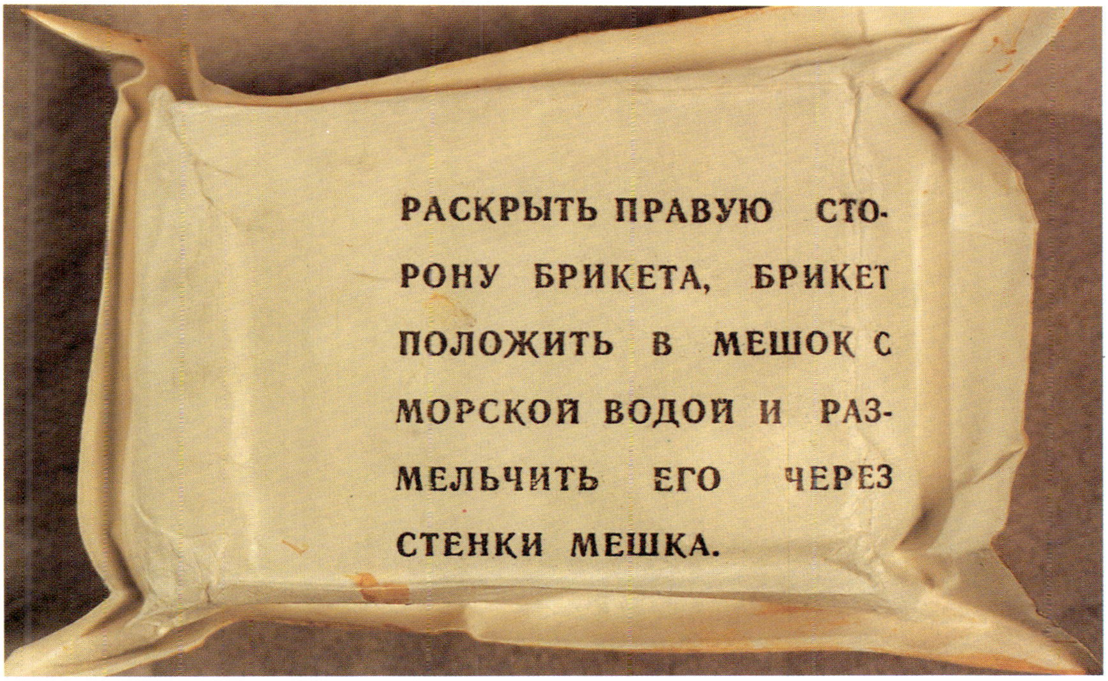

Desalting packet instructions, in short, read, "Open right side, empty into filter bag with seawater, and squeeze through filter."

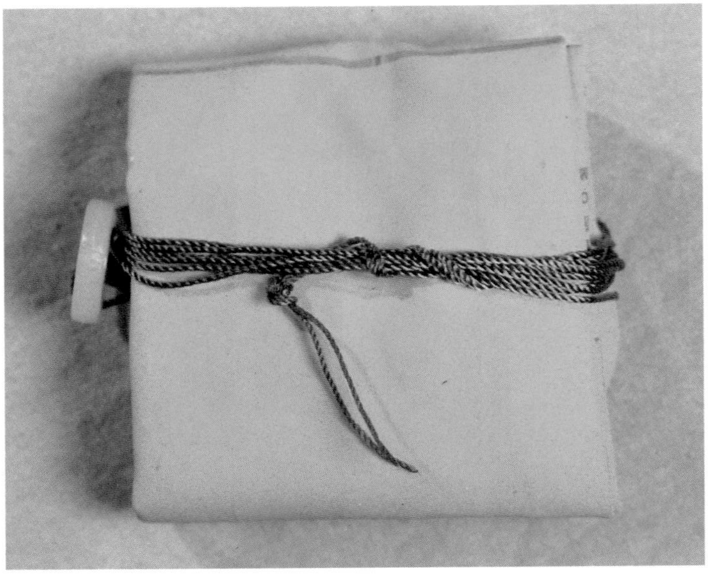

Desalting kit filter bag as stored in kit.

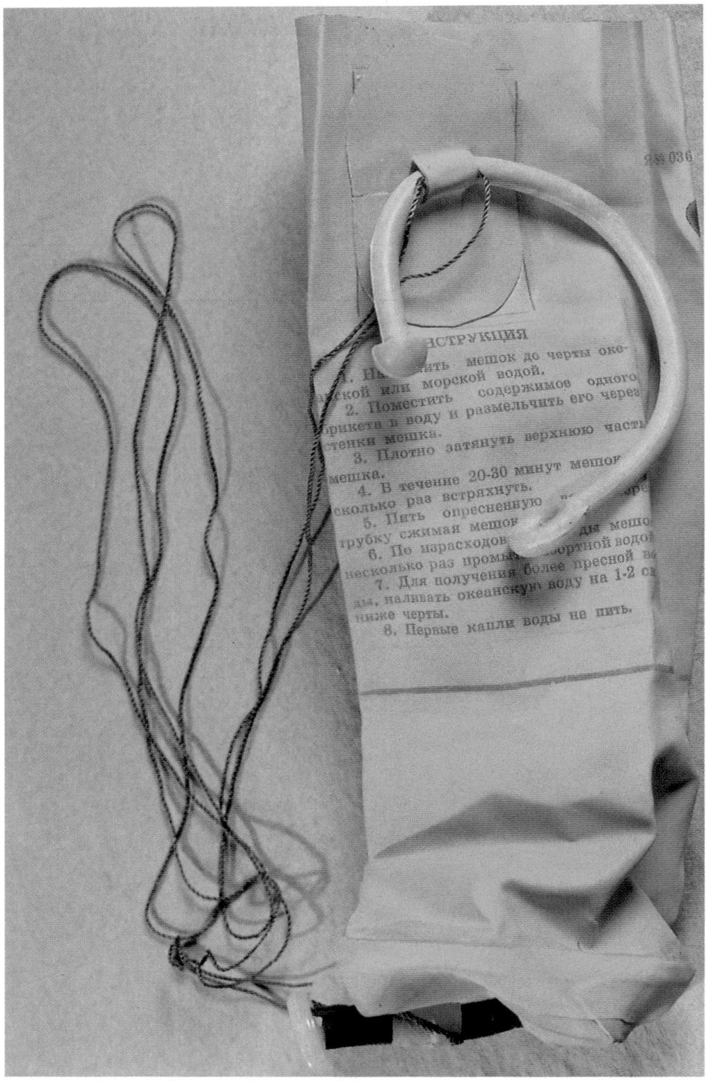

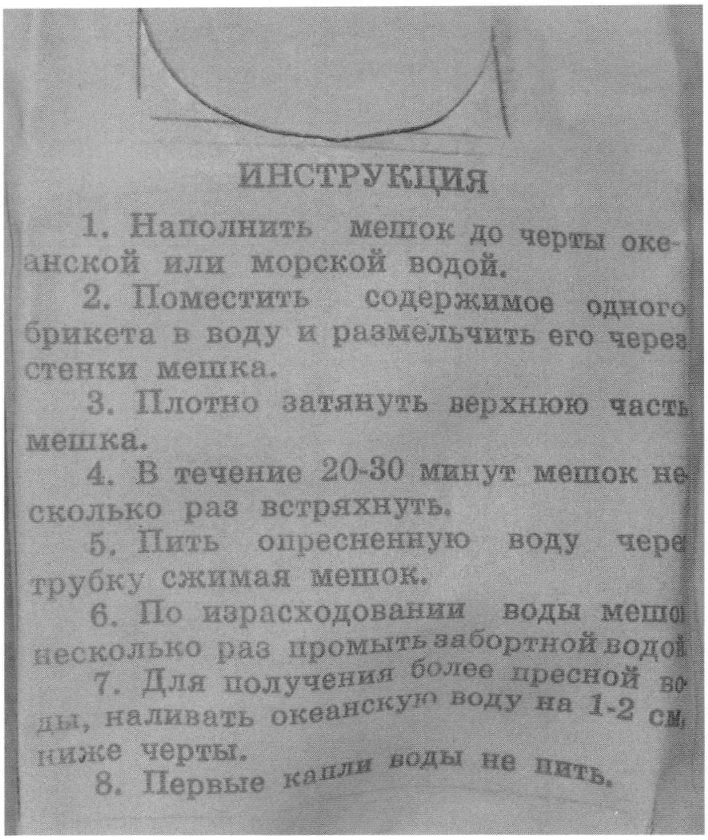

LEFT: Filter bag unfolded showing elastic band used to seal bag, filtered water tube, and instructions.

ABOVE: Instruction printed on filter bag read, in short: "**1**. Fill bag with sea water; **2**. Empty contents of one packet; **3**. Close and seal bag; **4**. Shake vigorously for 20-30 minutes; **5**. Drink from the bottom of bag by squeezing; **6**. Wash out bag with sea water before repeating procedure; **7**. Fill sea water only to line on bag for greater purity; **8**. The first drops will be salty."

NAZ-7M

The NAZ-7M is not a modified NAZ-7 but an entirely different kit. It is a soft type seat kit for use in ejection seat equipped aircraft, but is less extensive than the NAZ-7.

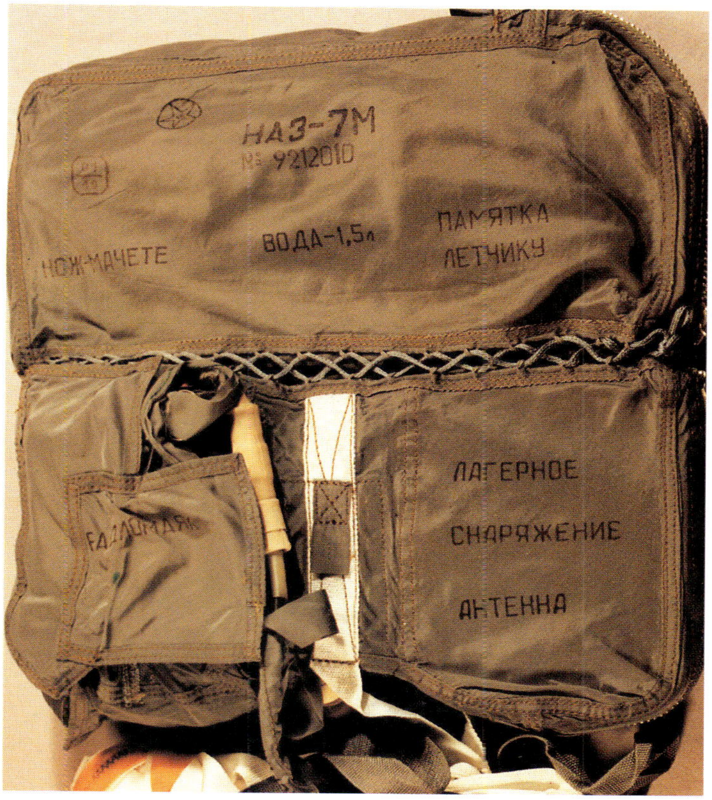

RIGHT: The NAZ-7M container is serial numbered and has four compartments which are clearly labeled with the major components: Left to right, top to bottom: "Knife-machete; 1.5 liter water container; aircrew survival manual; radio; survival equipment; antenna." White and orange nylon drop lines are shown at bottom.

BELOW: Contents of the NAZ-7M: (left to right, top to bottom): Deployment lines, "KOMAR-2MP" emergency radio beacon outfit; water container; machete; sunglasses; manual; "Priboy-2S" radio battery; survival kit container; dye marker.

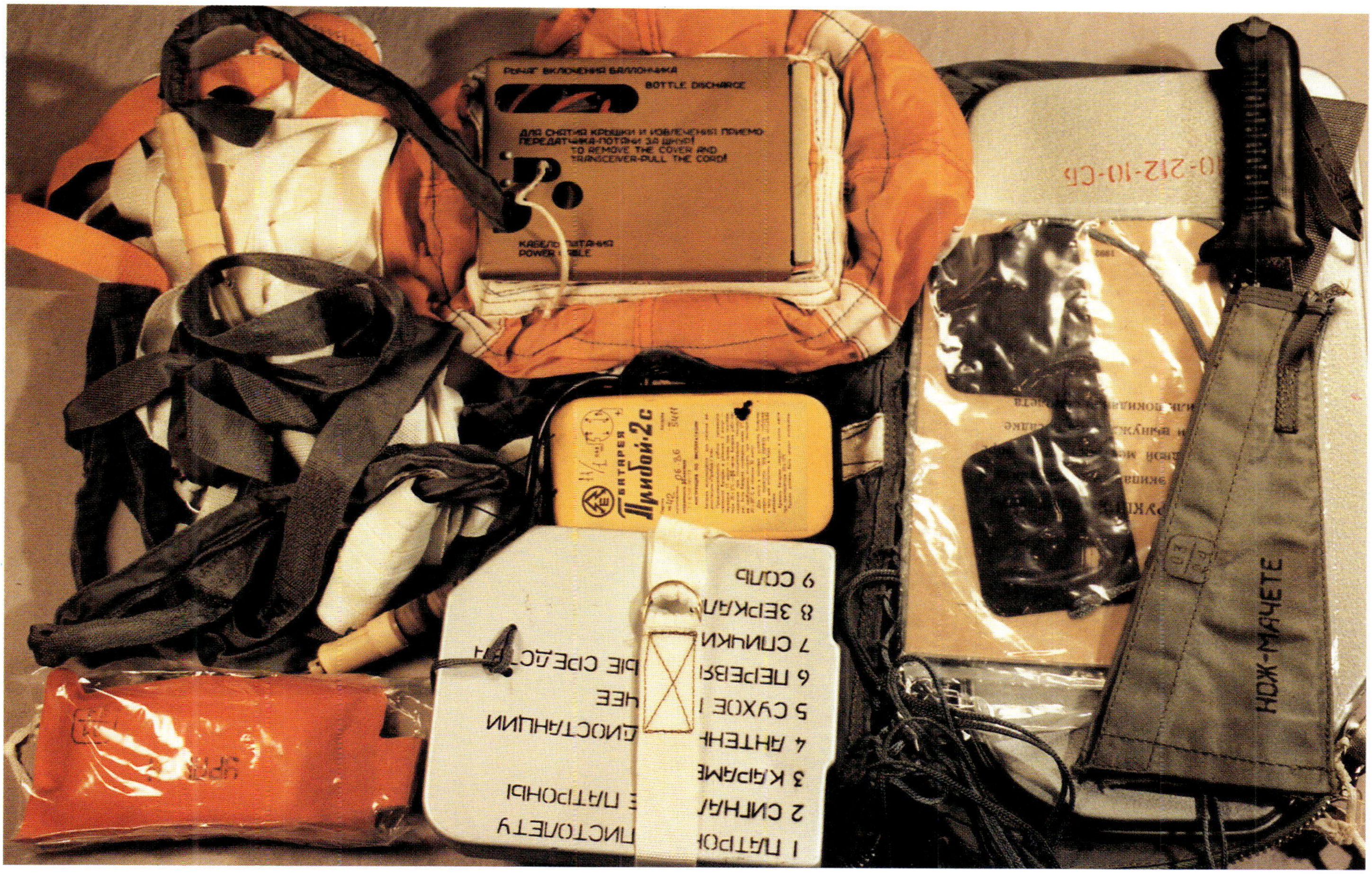

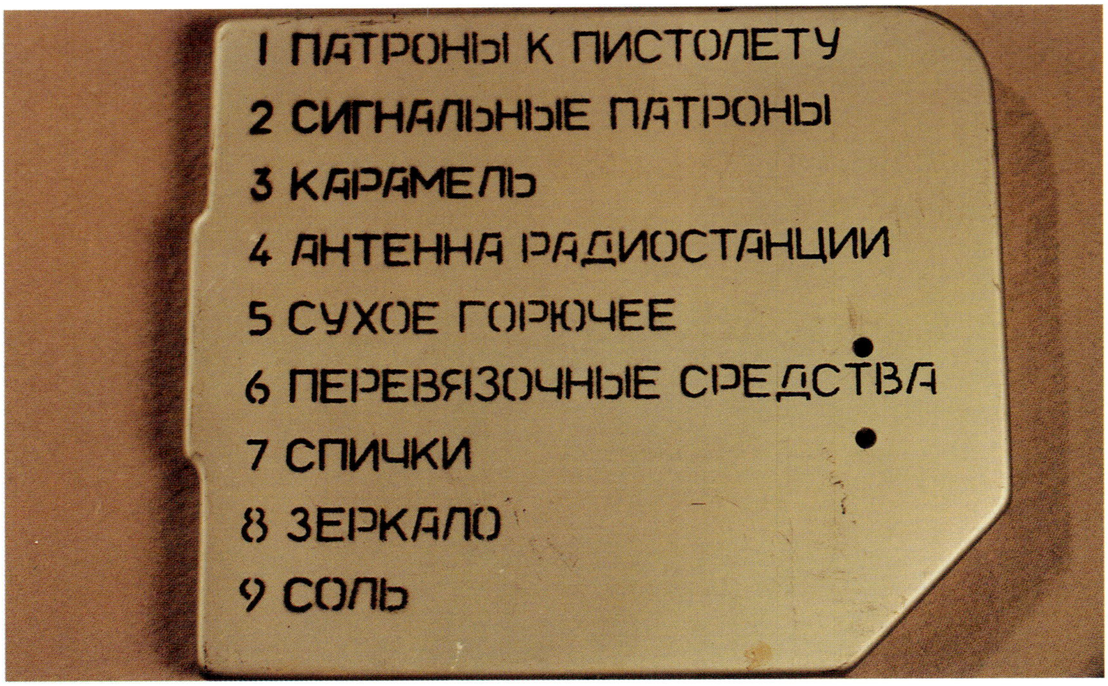

Survival kit container has contents listed on cover: "**1**. Pistol ammunition; **2**. Signal flare set; **3**. Candy; **4**. Radio antenna; **5**. Fire starters; **6**. Bandage/compress; 7. Matches; **8**. Signal mirror; **9**. Salt."

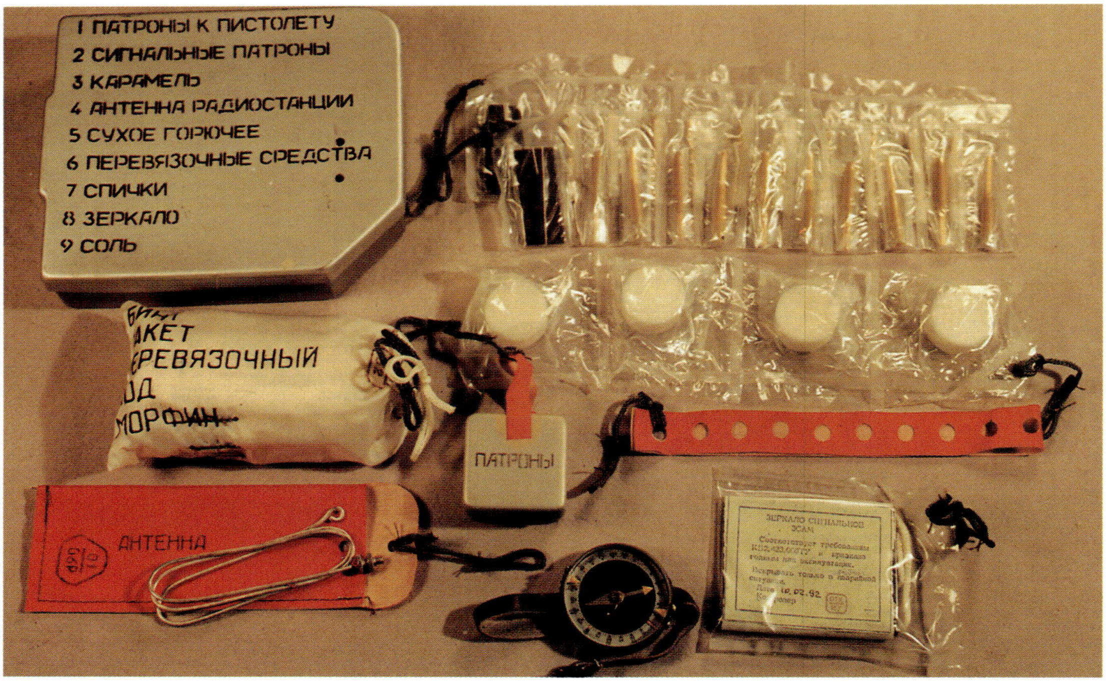

The actual contents of this NAZ-7M kit varies slightly from the list. (left to right, top to bottom): Container which converts to frying pan; 18 waterproof matches with striker; medical kit; fire starters; ammunition; orange strip is for 15mm. flare set as used in NAZ-7 and other kits; antenna; wrist compass; signal mirror.

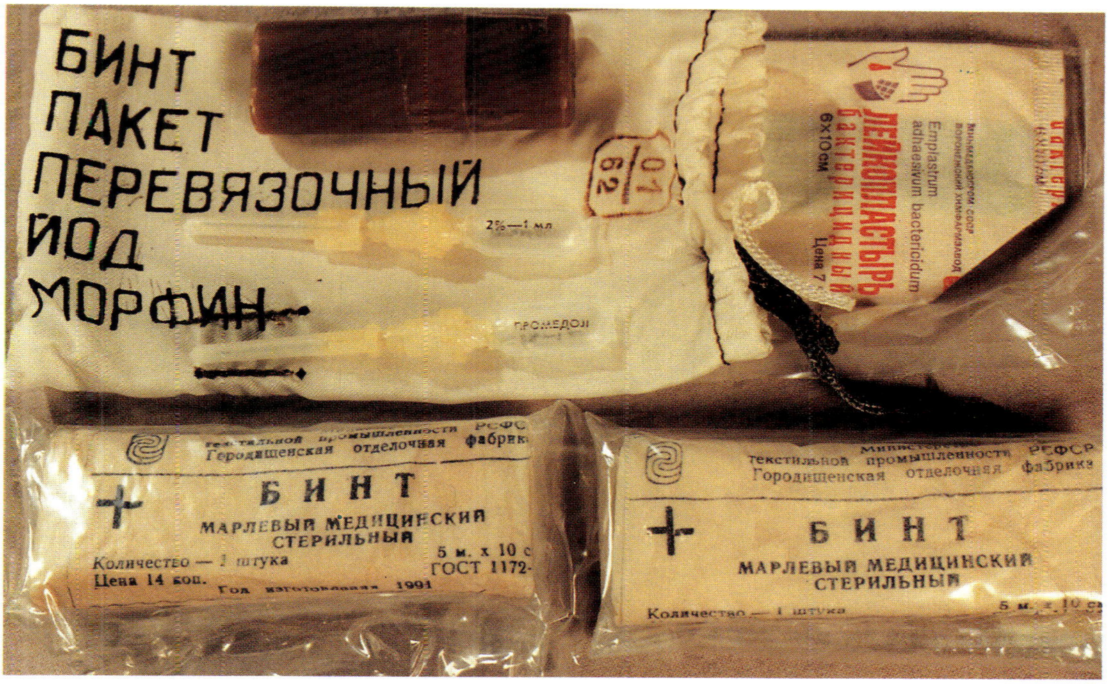

Medical kit contents list printed on bag: “Bandage, Compress, Iodine, Morphine.” Contents: Two iodine bottles in protective case; two Morphine syrettes; adhesive bandage two compresses.

Wrist compass in NAZ-7M is a military lensatic type which dates back to the 1930s, but works just fine. It is commonly used by all branches of the military and is used in all survival kits. Sights are mounted on moveable bezel ring. Pointer is locked in position by sliding clasp.

SOYUZ Spacecraft Survival Kit

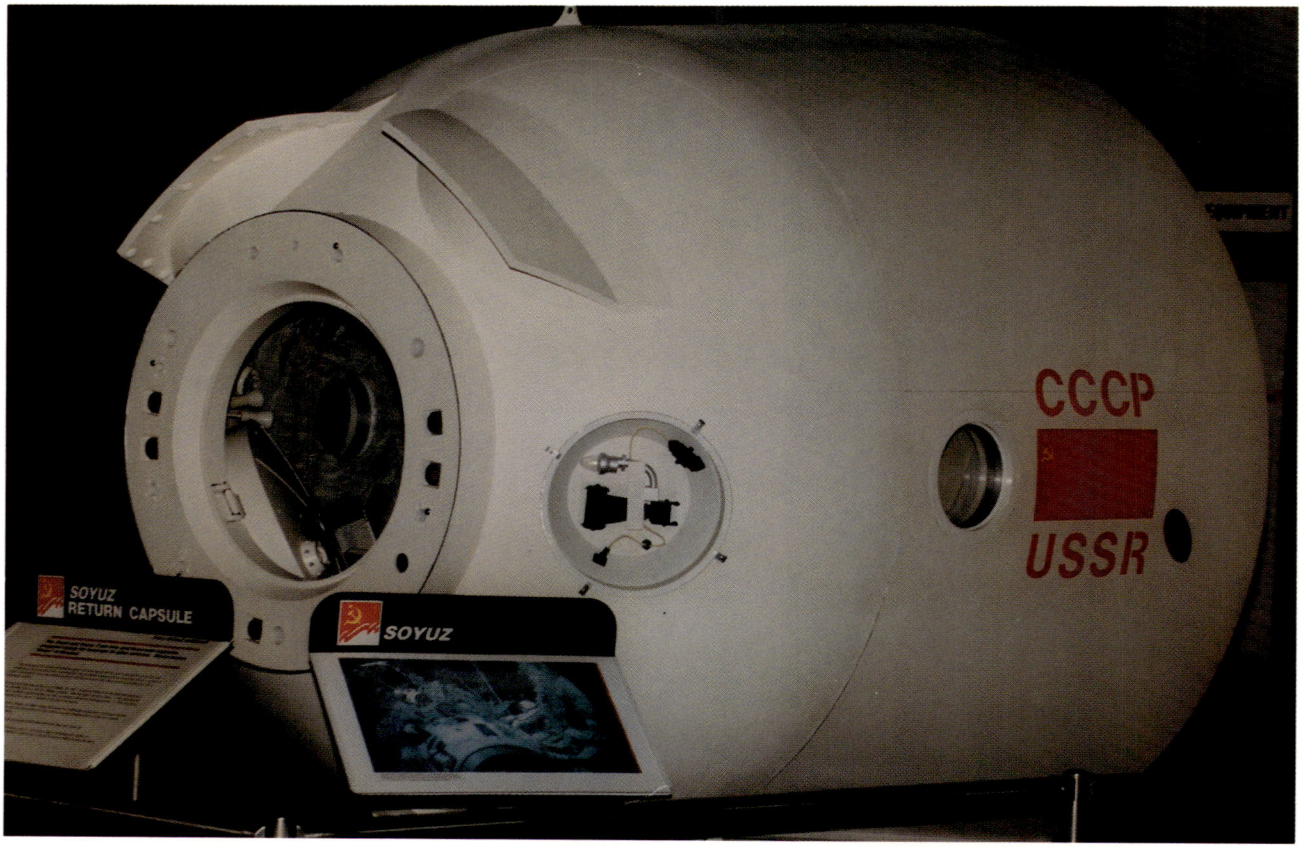

The Soyuz spacecraft accommodates three cosmonauts and is designed to land safely on land or water. Tiny errors in trajectory can cause a landing hundreds of miles off course.

NAZ-3

The NAZ-3 is contained in two orange triangular aluminum containers with gray canvas tops and zippers. They are stowed between the seats. The NAZ-3 is designed to serve the three cosmonauts for 72 hours and includes: (left to right, top to bottom): Makarov pistol and ammo; wrist compass; 18 waterproof matches with striker; machete; fishing kit; strobe light with spare battery; 8 fire starters; folding knife; antenna; 3 pair wool gloves; signal mirror; NAZ-7M type medical kit; penlight; R-855-YM or R-855-A1 radio; two "Priboy 2S" radio batteries; three wool balaclava hoods. Not shown are containers, three PSND hand-held flares; 15mm flare set; whistle; sewing kit; insect repellent; wire saw; rations; and 2-liter water container.

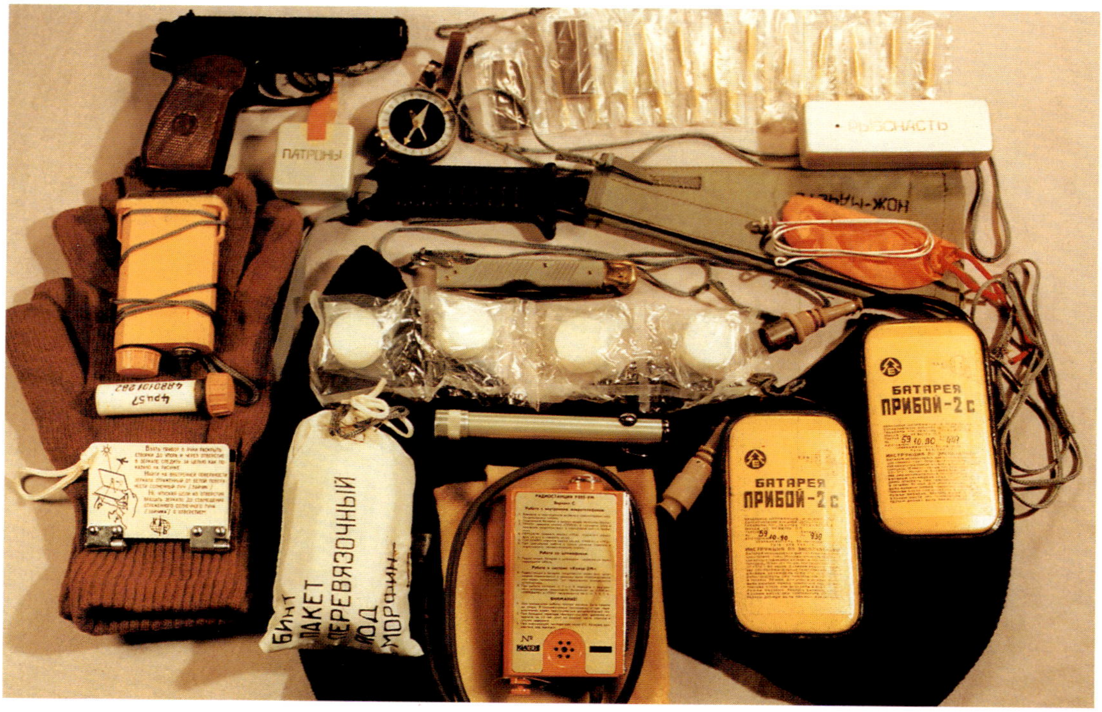

Helicopter Survival Vest

NAZ-I

The NAZ-I was designed and developed for combat helicopter crews during the war in Afghanistan, primarily as a self-defense measure as crews stood little chance of surviving at the hands of their adversary. Manufactured of the same Nomex type material as used in the VKK-6M series high altitude partial-pressure suit, the NAZ-I is an unusual gray-green color with gray and tan detailing. It is often worn with the camouflage flightsuit.

An Mi-24 "HIND" crew in Afghanistan wearing NAZ-I vest. 5.45mm AKR "Krinkov" carbine used by crews for self defense is seen in the lower left.

ABOVE LEFT: The rear of the vest holds pouches for a signal mirror, two 30-round "Krinkov" magazines, and a map pocket (center, bottom).

ABOVE RIGHT: Available to aircrew in one size only, there are four lace-adjustment locations: each side and each shoulder.

RIGHT: Label of NAZ-I vest shows individual serial number printed in the collar which is registered to the crewman for identification.

The left side of the vest has pouches for specific items: (left to right, top to bottom): Folding knife or 15mm flare set; signal mirror; Makarov 9x18mm pistol; extra pistol magazine; 30-round magazine; strobe light with extra battery; and small fishing kit. The fishing kit and MEM-76M1 strobe light are for domestic use. In combat circumstances, two PSND hand-held flares would be carried in this pouch.

The right side pouches contain: (left to right, top to bottom): General pouch with wire saw; 9 waterproof matches with striker; wrist compass; and whistle; compress and medical kit which can be accessed from the top or bottom of the pouch for emergencies. 30-round magazine; R-855YM radio; "Priboy-2S" battery; fishing line and antenna; 30-round magazine.

The left inside pocket contains a water bag, penlight, and smaller version manual, all stored in a plastic bag.

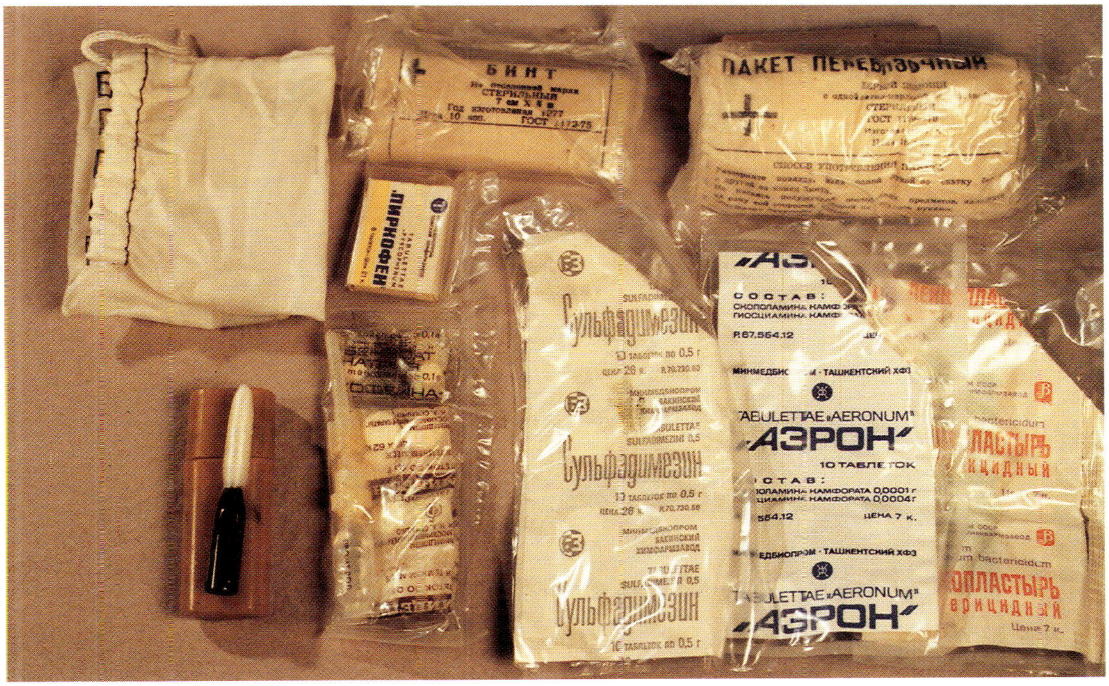

The NAZ-I medical kit includes: (left to right, top to bottom): Storage bag; gauze bandage; compress; 6 caffeine pills; 6 "Perkafine" pills; iodine with protective case; Morphine syrette; 10 antibiotic pills; 10 Sulfide pills; 10 aspirin tablets; adhesive bandage.

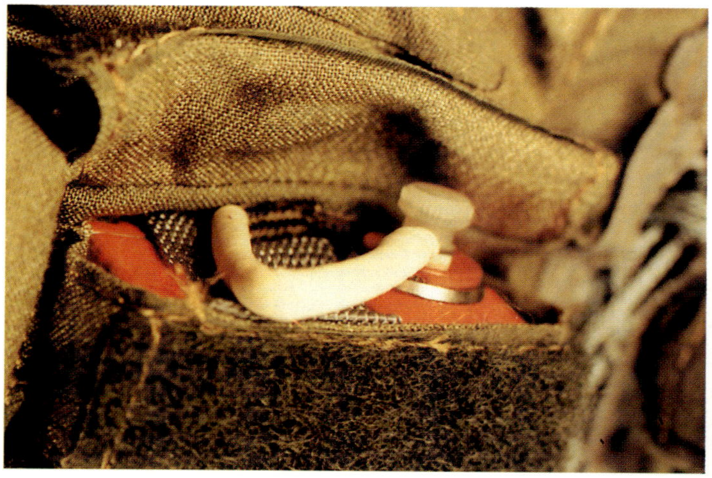

A unique feature of the NAZ-I is the built-in radio antenna allowing operation in the "locating-tone" mode while being worn. The antenna is connected to the radio in the pouch.

The antenna extends from the bottom of the radio pouch up inside the right side of the vest to the collar area.

Flotation Devices

ASZ-63P

The ASZ-63P is a life preserver designed for use on aircraft without ejection seats. It is worn over the head and simply tied around the waist.

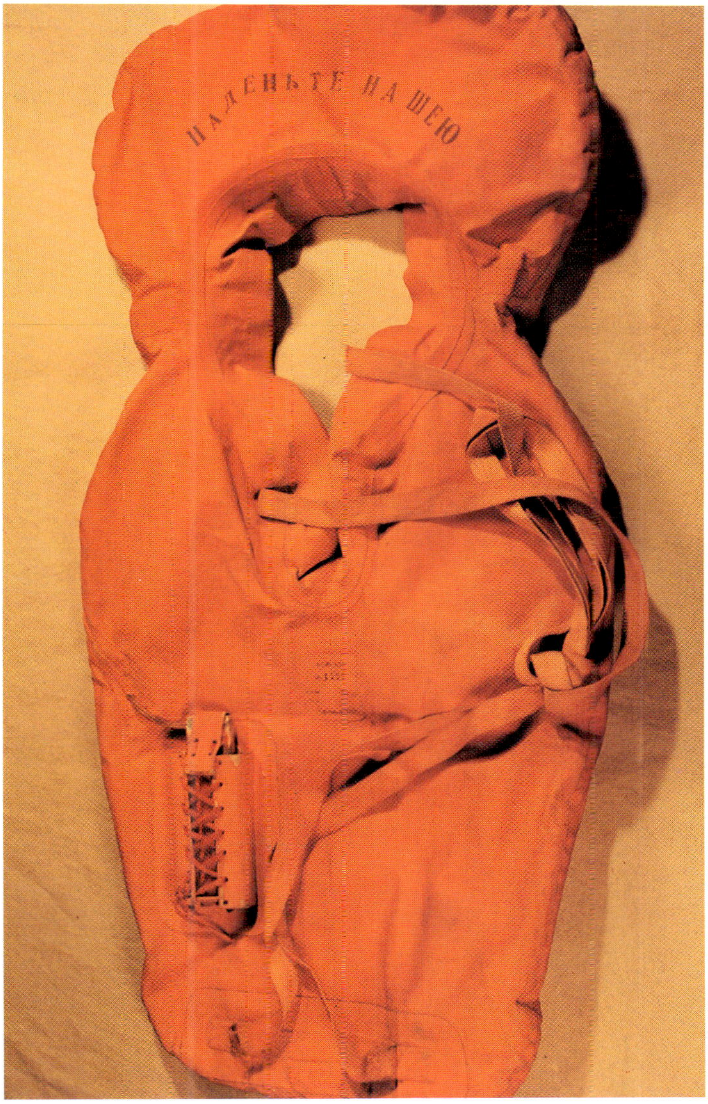

The underside of the ASZ-63P shows the water activated battery and waist straps. Words at the top state: "Do Not Puncture."

On the front, a black CO_2 activation cartridge can be seen along with a pocket and whistle; light; and two manual inflation valves.

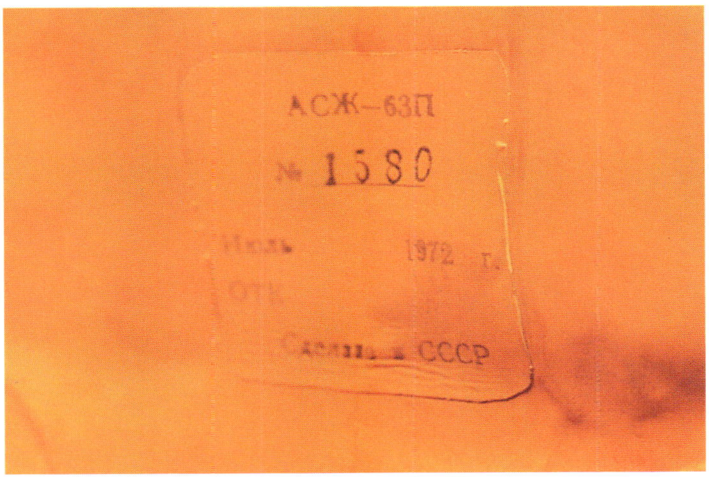

ASZ-63P label

ASZ-58

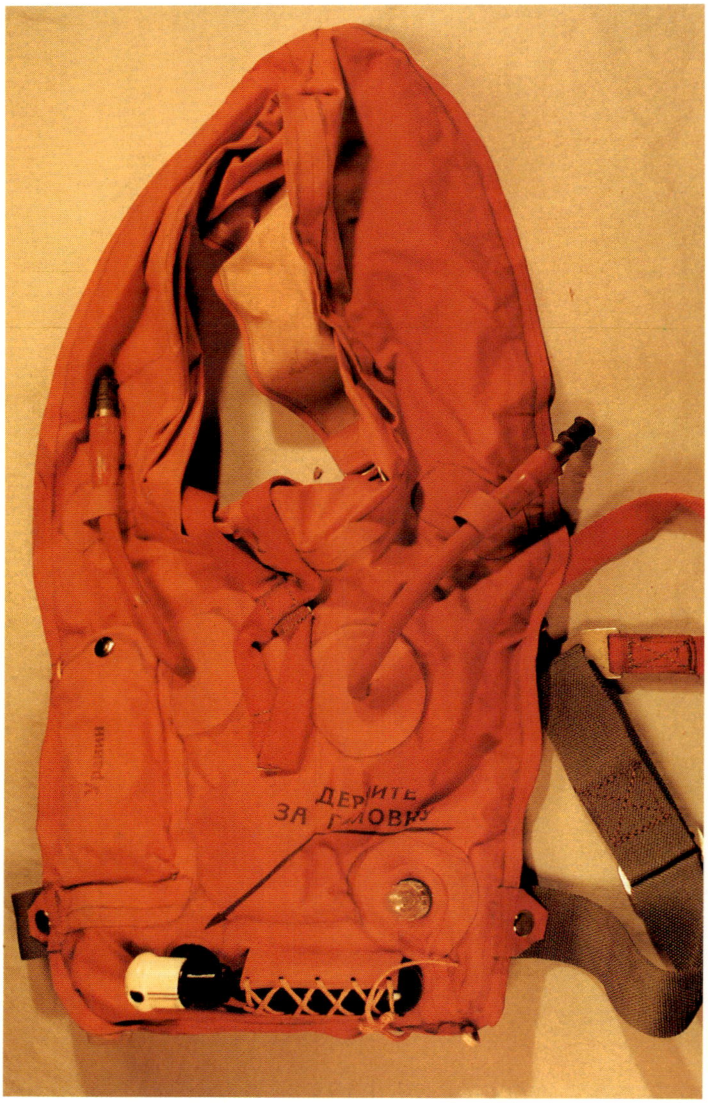

The ASZ-58 life preserver is designed for use in any type aircraft, primarily for over water use. The front of the ASZ-58 contains a dye marker; CO_2 activation cartridge; light; two manual inflation valves; and rescue/extraction harness attachment point.

The extraction harness loop is held in place by snaps until needed. Dye marker pouch can be clearly seen on left.

The underside of the ASZ-58 shows the water activated battery; life raft clip; whistle; and signal mirror. The rescue/extraction harness is clearly shown.

ASZ-58 label

Storage bag

ASP-74

The ASP-74 is an underarm type life preserver designed specifically for ejection seat equipped aircraft. It is also used by helicopter crews and high altitude pilots. The bright blue units (left) are worn in pairs around the waist on a belt. When inflated (right), each unit supports the airman under the arms and can be attached together. The ASP-74 is inflated by a CO_2 cartridge or manually.

ABOVE: Each ASP-74 unit is serial numbered. RIGHT ASP-74 storage bag.

ASR-35 Life Raft

The ASR-35 is a one man life raft designed for use with all types of aircraft but primarily single or dual seat aircraft. The life raft has many uses besides in the water (see Chapter 3).

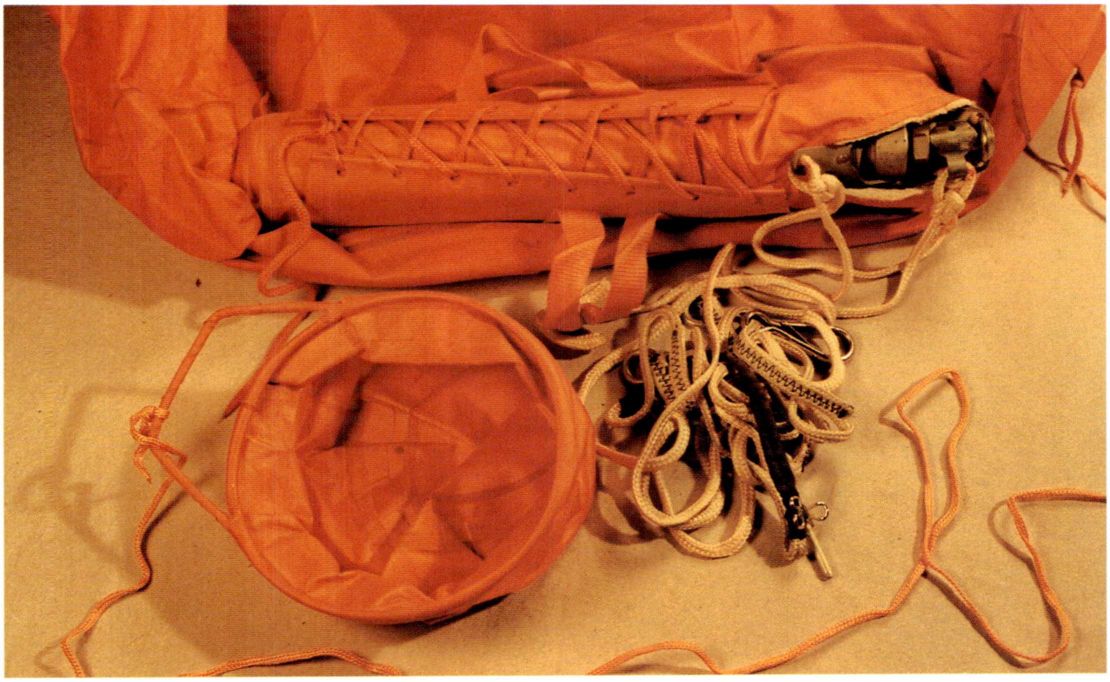

The raft is inflated by way of a standard CO_2 cartridge system shown in its storage pouch. A collapsible bailing bucket is standard issue.

To provide additional inflation, a bellows type hand pump is built-in. The white material is a "sea anchor" and used to stabilize the raft.

Four "bullet" type life raft hole plugs are carried in bag. Every item is tied to raft for security.

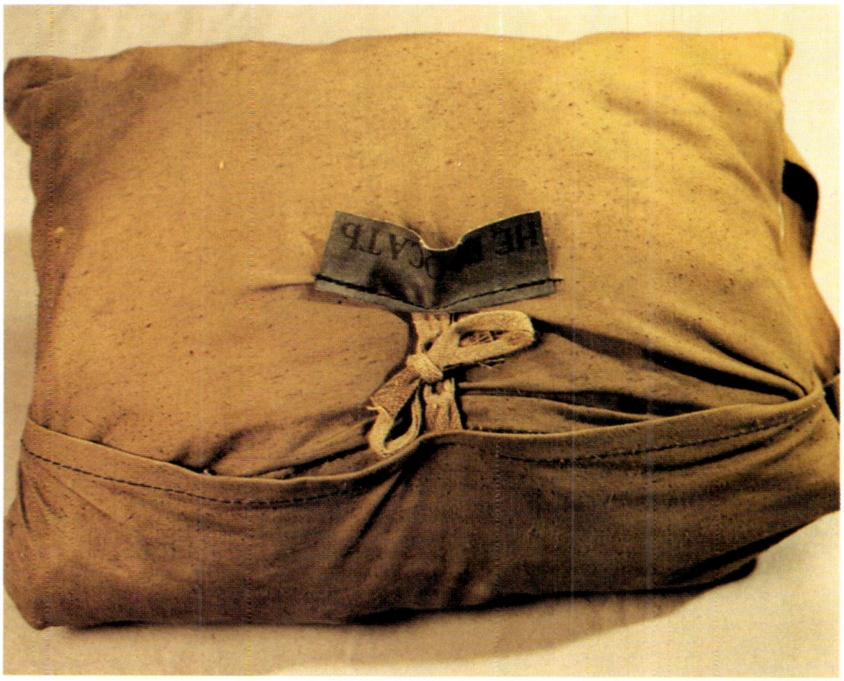

Storage bag carries warning tag: "Don't Puncture."

Exposure Suits

Although conventional exposure suits are technically considered flight clothing and protect the wearer from water, Russian suits offer a complex combination of functions which do much more and contribute greatly to overall survival. They are worn under harsh arctic conditions for warmth as well as over water, and by all aircrews, from helicopters to high altitude fighters. Their overall design and construction exhibit many of the same characteristics as cosmonaut launch and re-entry full pressure suits.

VMSK-2

First issued in 1963, the VMSK-2 combines total water immersion protection with micro-climate heating, cooling, and ventilation. Not unlike a spacesuit, venting air is piped from a cockpit system throughout the suit. Shown here with a GSh-6M high altitude pressure helmet. Silver disks on sleeves are water tight ventilation control valves. Wrists are sealed by a rubber cuff.

The micro-climate layer of the VMSK-2 is a well insulated coverall with ventilation tubing running throughout. The system is attached to the outer cover by two connectors seen at waist level.

RIGHT: Special boots are connected and sealed to the main cover with interlocking heavy rubber flanges and collars.

TWO BELOW: A feature shared by the VMSK-2 with the very first cosmonaut suit – the SK-1 – is an integrated life preserver mounted on the back. This system frees the suit of a bulky external life preserver which, given the weight of the suit, would need to be quite large.

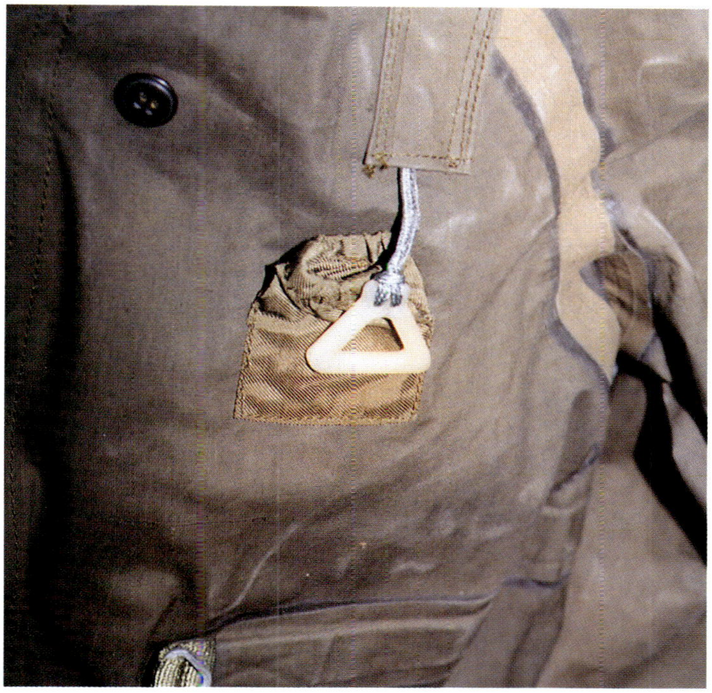

LEFT: The floatation system is activated by a pull cord located on the upper left chest, the same as on the SK-1.

VMSK-2 label with serial number and size "R-5."

BELOW LEFT: The floatation unit has "wings" which wrap around under the arms and link together in front.

BELOW RIGHT: The SK-1 cosmonaut suit showing floatation backpack.

VMSK-4

The VMSK-4 is in current use, shown here with ASP-74 life preservers. Bright orange color aids rescue.

Like the VMSK-2, the inner micro-climate coverall is heavily insulated and has ventilation tubing throughout.

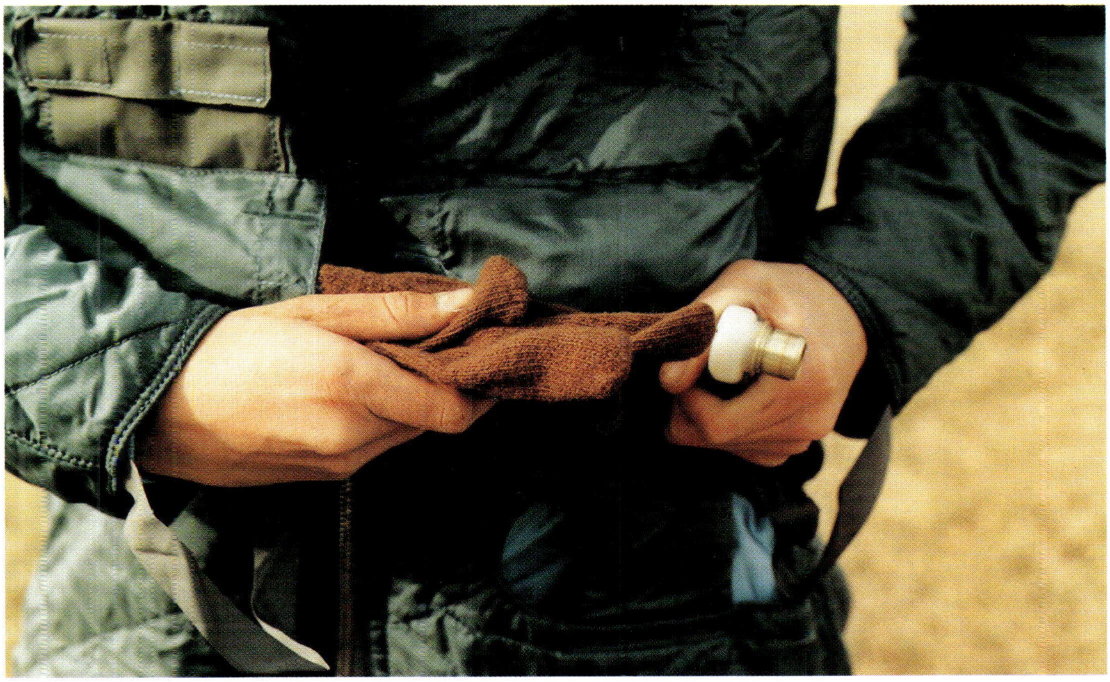

Wool gloves are stored in the chest pouches. Single ventilation connector for outer cover is on the right.

Label shows serial number and size "R-5."

The right sleeve of the VMSK-4 has a signal mirror built in with a matching cover held in place by Velcro. The mirror also permits a pilot wearing a high altitude pressure helmet to inspect his suit/helmet/visor connection. This feature is also shared by cosmonaut suits.

Inside the left collar is a pouch for a spare Makarov pistol magazine. The left chest pocket (not shown) is actually a holster with lanyard for a Makarov. Most all Russian flight suits have built in pistol holsters.

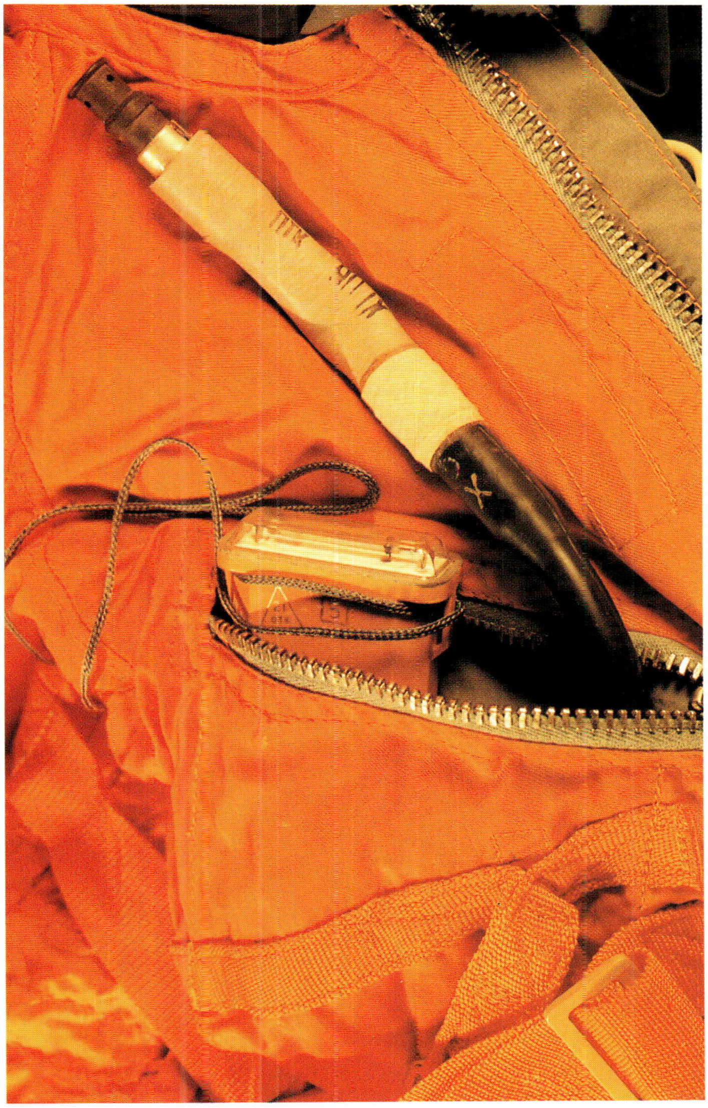

The right chest pocket carries a MEM-76M1 strobe light and manual inflation valve.

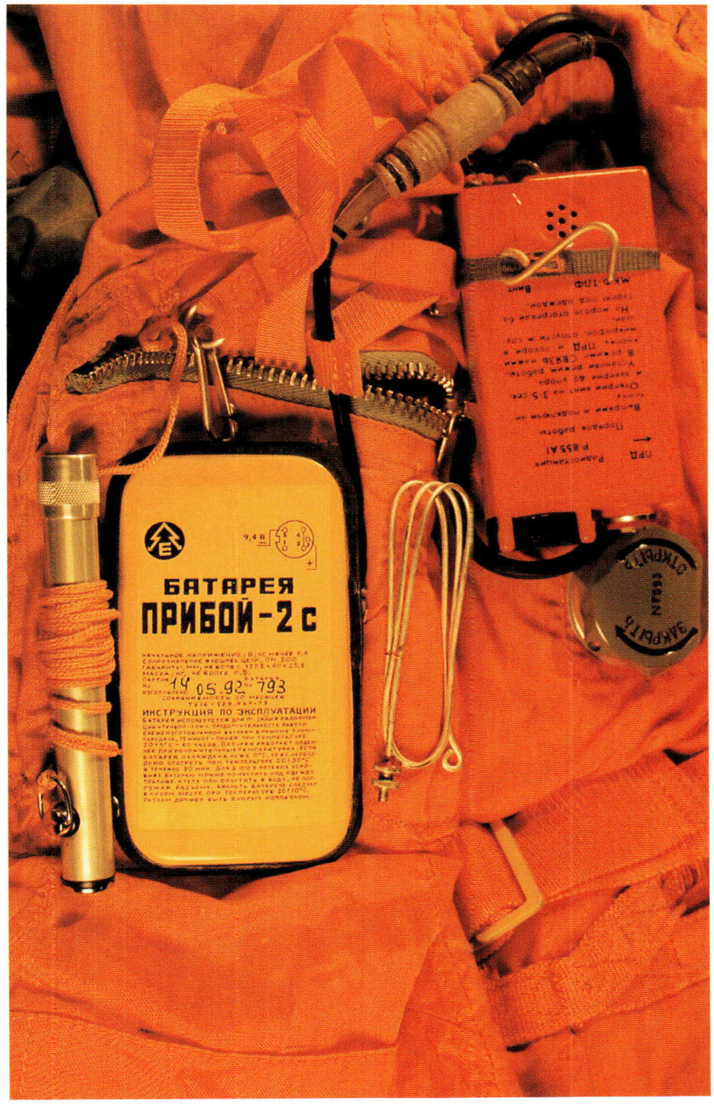

The right leg pocket of the VMSK-4 is designed to carry an R-855A1 radio with battery and antenna, along with a penlight.

The VMSK-4 is issued with a matching orange neck skirt for the GSh-6AA high altitude helmet and a repair kit.

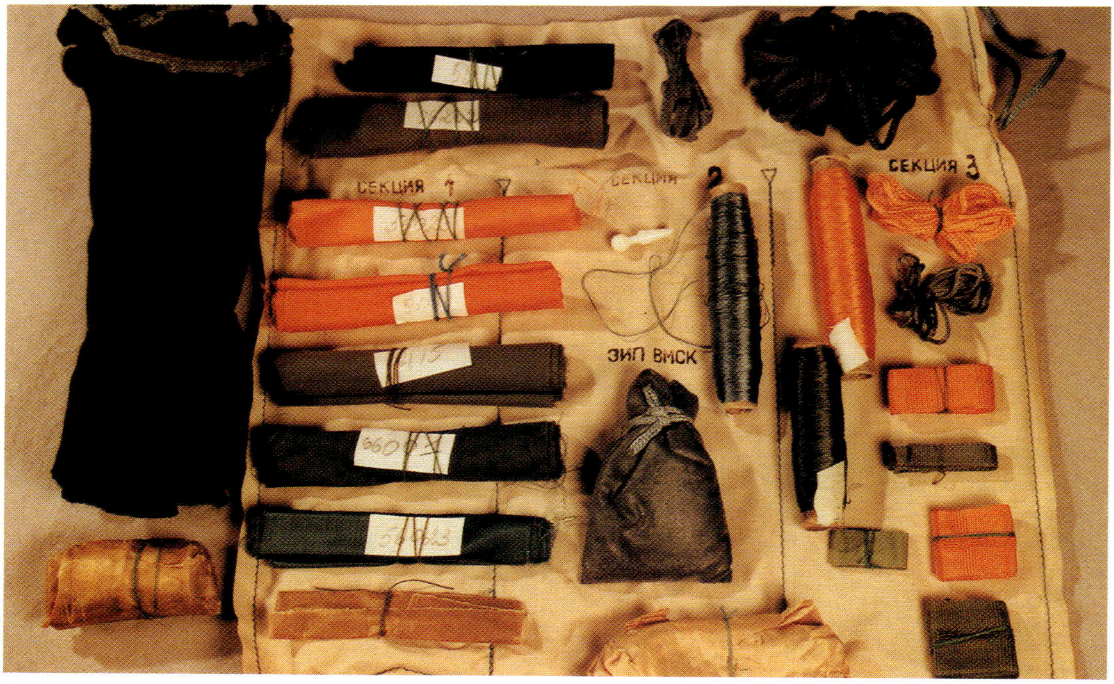

The repair kit for the VMSK-4 is very extensive. It includes replacement wool collar and cuffs; elastic bands; donning powder (in bag at center); material samples for every part of the suit; thread for the same; as well as samples of every strap and cord. Sewing needles are in wrapping (lower left).

SOKOL III

This SOKOL III ("Falcon") full-pressure suit was reportedly designed for the Soviet "Buran" space shuttle program. It also may be a new type of high altitude suit. Given its design features, it is possibly both. It has been included here for its unique and apparent war time survival features. Notably first, is the camouflage outer cover. An unusual feature for a spacesuit, it would help conceal the wearer, but also aid in concealing the discarded yet bulky suit. RIGHT: The right leg of the SOKOL III has specific pockets for (left to right): Folding knife; Makarov pistol; extra magazine; R-855A1 radio, antenna, and battery.

Makarov, magazine, and folding knife each have a separate pocket and retention cord.

Radio, battery, antenna, and straps are sealed in foam-padded plastic bag in lower leg pocket.

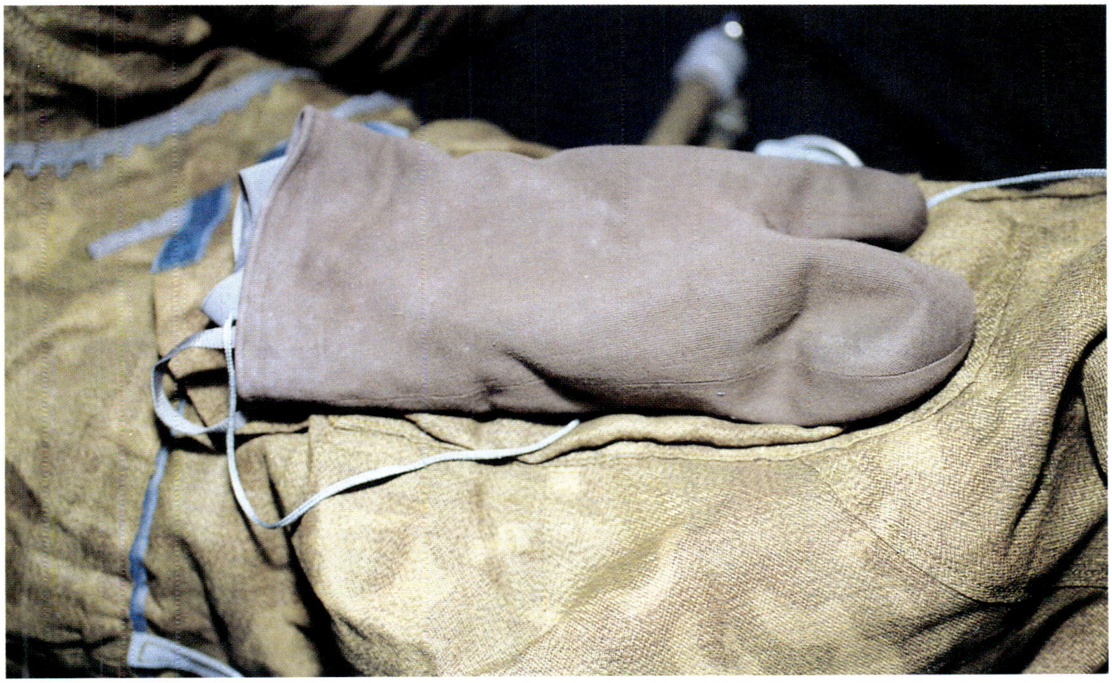

Water tight insulated mittens are carried in pockets located in each hip of the suit. These are the same as those carried in the VMSK-4.

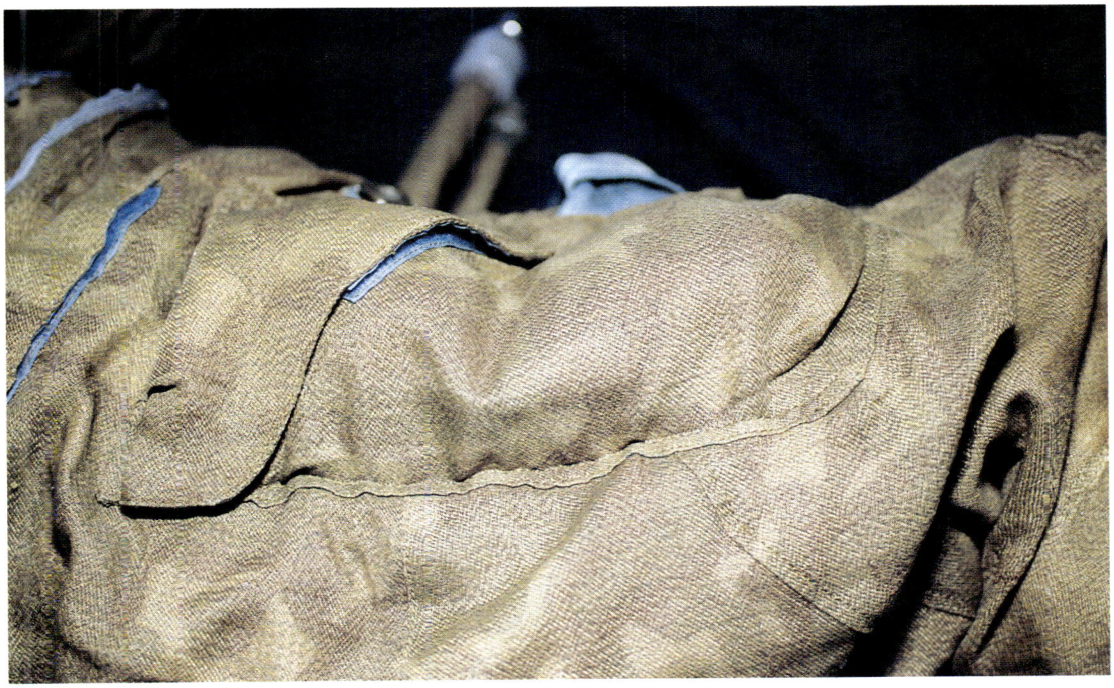

Survival Radios

R-855U

A variety of R-855 series radios and "Priboy" batteries are used in all types of kits and survival applications.

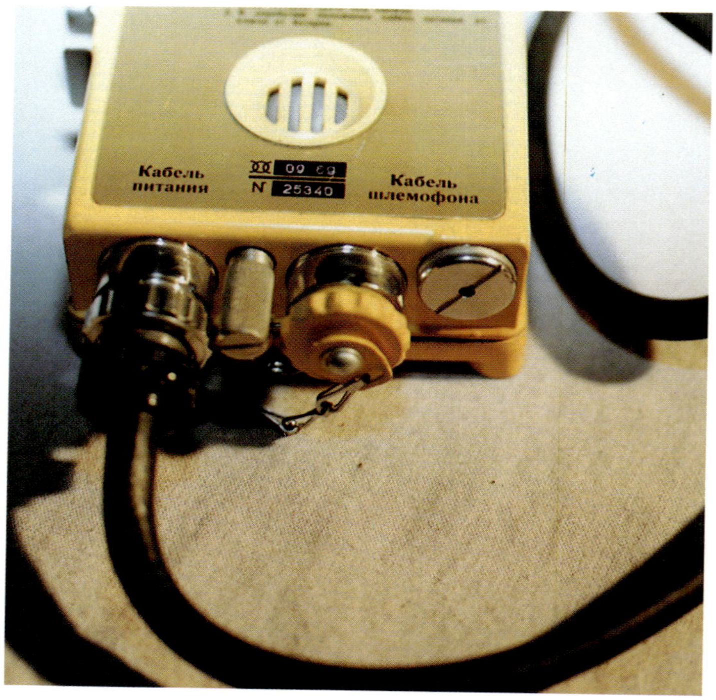

The R-855U radio was introduced in the mid-1960s and is still found in some locations. It has no volume control and the microphone and speaker are shared. As with all R-855 series radios, the battery is connected by way of a cord. This design permits the radio to be used in arctic conditions while keeping the battery warm under clothing. The R-855U uses a telescoping antenna. RIGHT: Threaded caps protect the radio from the elements. Cap shown protects plug which connects radio to flight helmet for auxiliary use.

Operating instructions are clearly listed on the front of the R-855U. These include how to: "Connect battery; extend antenna; operate microphone; operate locating beacon mode; warnings to not operate too long and to keep battery warm." Radio is dated September, 1969; Serial number 25340.

Control buttons can be locked into either on or off positions by sliding catches on the top and bottom. All R-855 radios are tuned only to the international military distress channel 243.0 UHF.

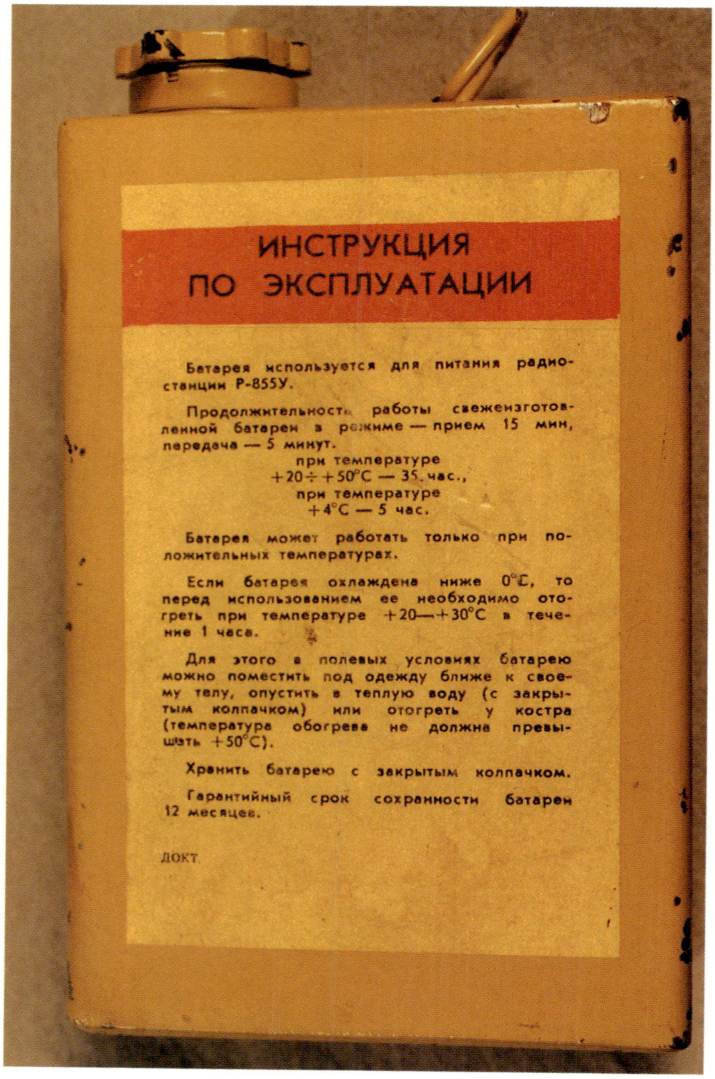

The R-855U uses a "Priboy-1" battery. A plastic cap protects the connection plug until needed. The instructions on the back lists most importantly: "Operate for 15 minutes at a time for the first 5 hours of need. Expected battery life based on temperature: 20 to 50 degrees C.= 35 hours; 4 degrees C.= 5 hours." Battery is dated November, 1986.

R-855UM

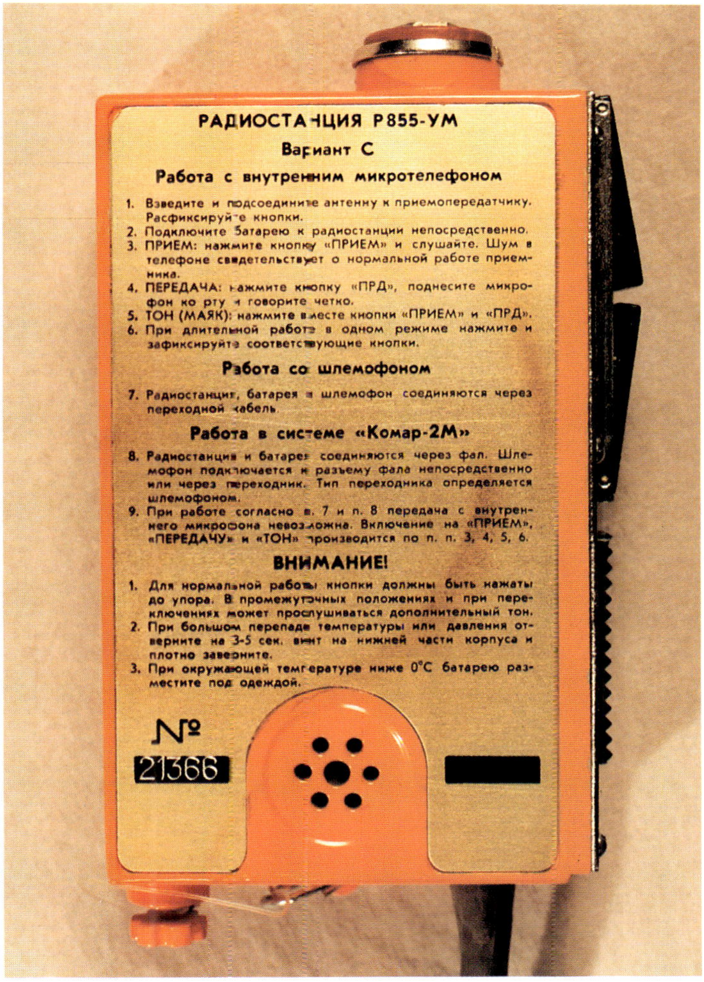

The R-855UM is much smaller that the R-855U with earlier versions painted yellow. It has no volume control and the microphone and speaker are shared. Operating instructions are similar to the R-855U.

The "Priboy-2S" battery is much smaller than the "Priboy-1" but offers similar performance. The connecting plug has a protective cap in place. It is a remote, 9.4 volt model dated May, 1992.

Operating controls are simple: To receive, the black button on top is depressed; to transmit voice, black button in the middle is depressed; to transmit in "beacon" mode, middle button is depressed and lower switch is slid up, locking it down.

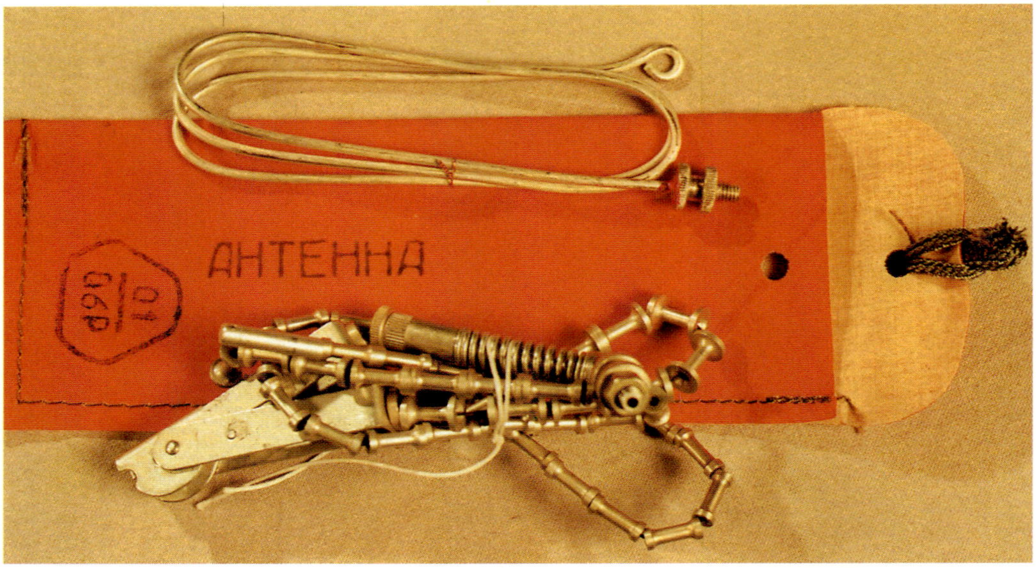

Two types of antennas are used with the R-855UM radio. One is a simple aluminum wire which extends to the tuned length of 60cm. and threads into the top of the radio (top). The other type is a very complex articulated design made of a series of aluminum segments connected by a thin stainless steel wire. This allows for a very compact and rugged antenna.

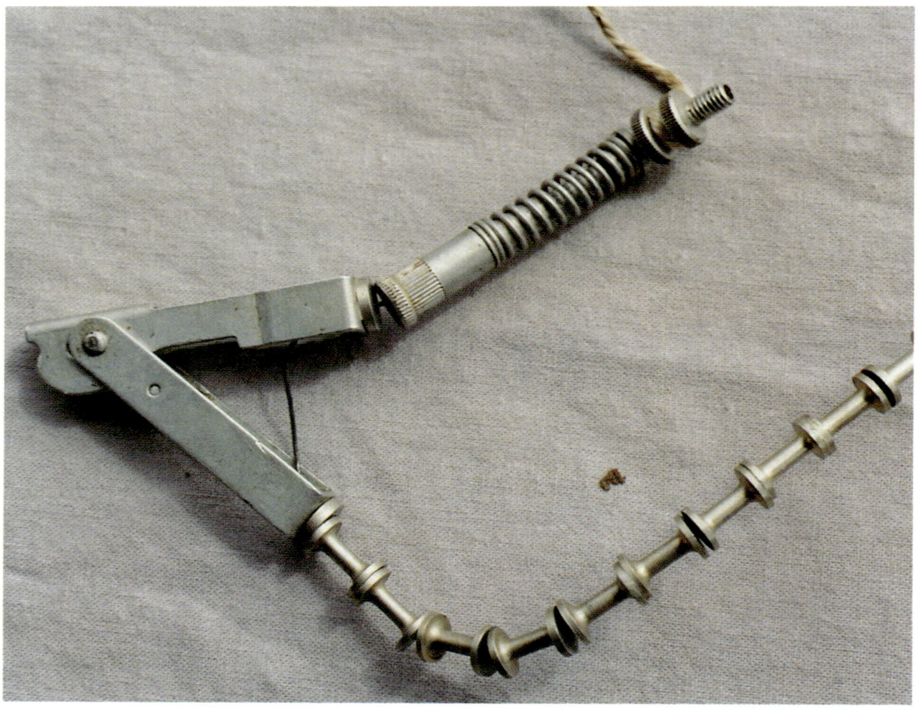

When the hinged bracket is straightened, the wire is tensioned and the antenna is extended to the same tuned length of 60cm.

"KOMAR-2MP"

The "KOMAR-2MP" is an emergency locating radio beacon outfit which is automatically deployed from the NAZ-7M and other kits. The heart of the outfit is a bright orange balloon which is inflated with a CO_2 cartridge and serves three main functions: It allows the outfit to float; an antenna mounted inside is extended and maintained in a vertical position; the bright color and shape aid in rescue. The "KOMAR-2MP" uses the R-855UM radio mounted in the base. It can be removed and used in a conventional manner as an antenna and straps are included. Drop lines are in upper right.

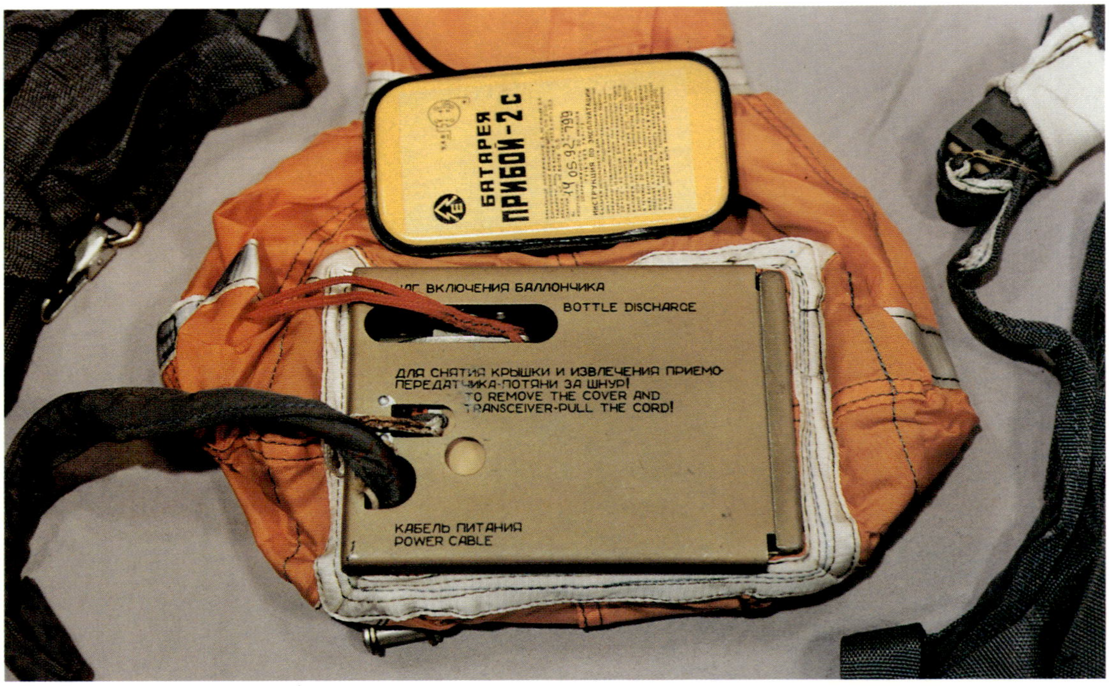

The base of the unit has Russian and English instructions; English being the international aviation language.

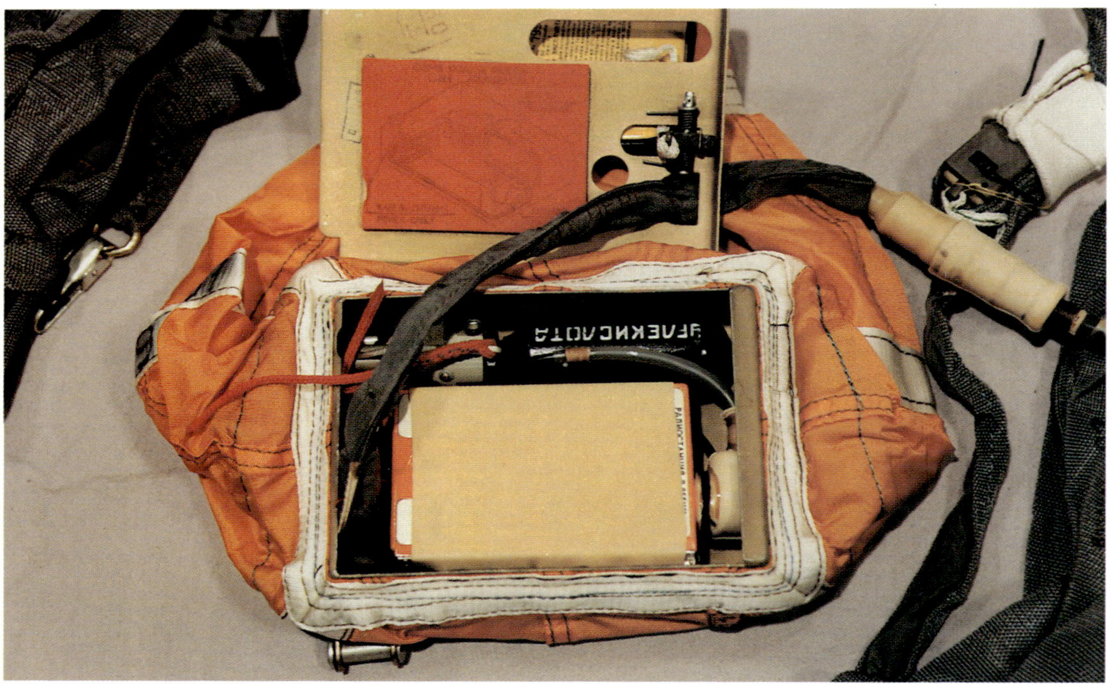

Inside the base is the radio in a protective rubber cover and the CO_2 cartridge.

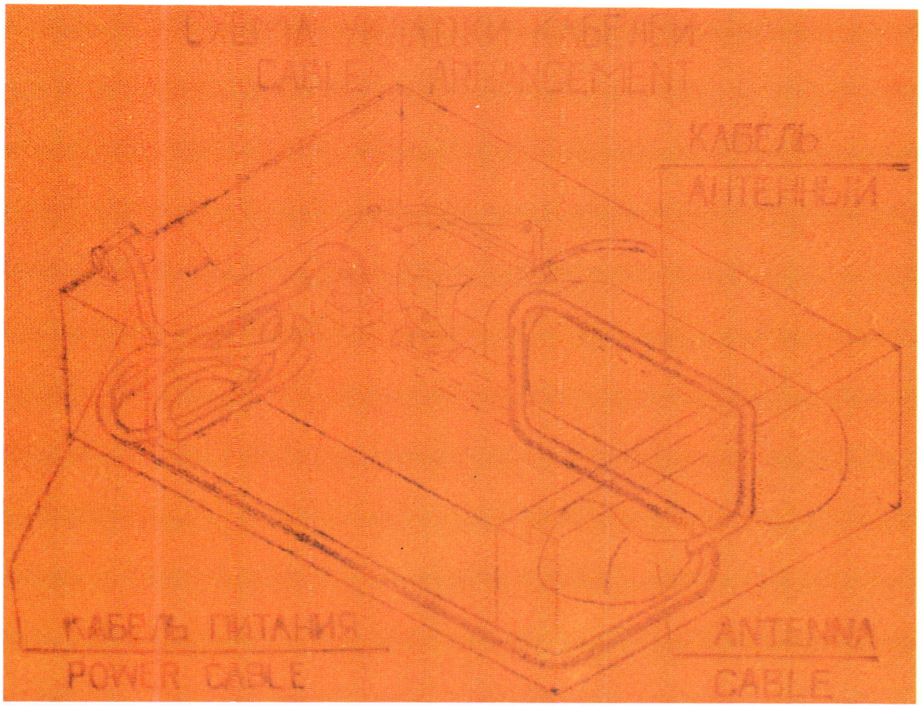

Instructions on the inside of the cover are also bi-lingual.

The "KOMAR-2MP" is activated by this battery switch located in the drop line. When the line is extended, the switch is activated, turning on the system.

The storage bag has serial number.

R-855A1

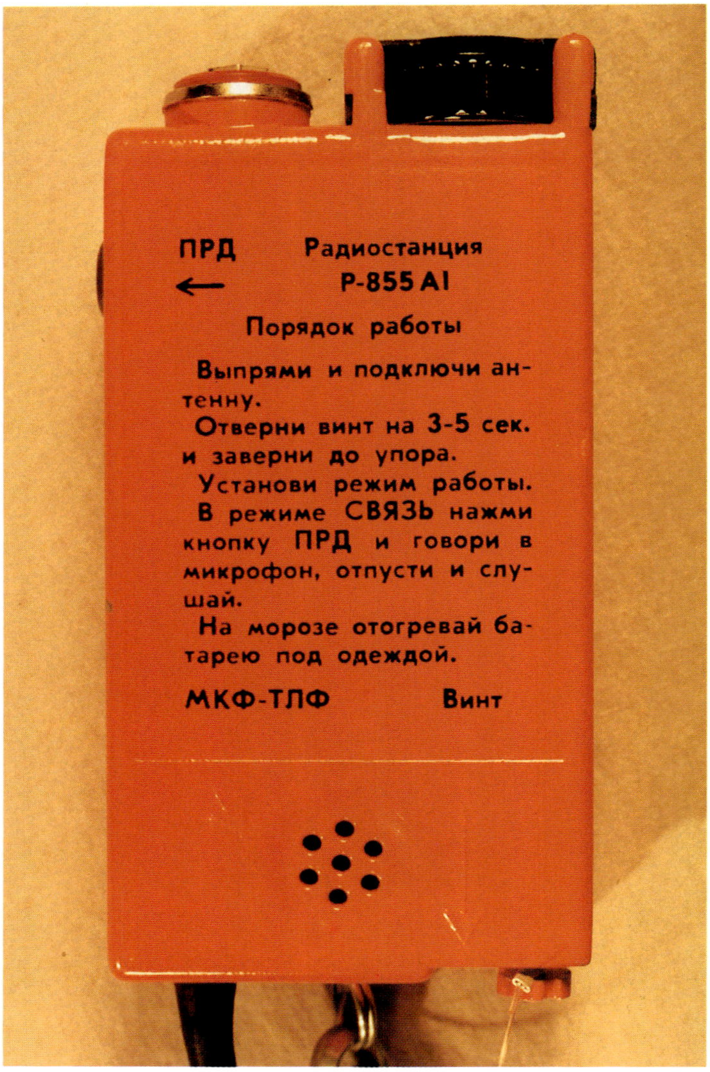

The R-855A1 is the newest type. It has no volume control, and simplified instructions.

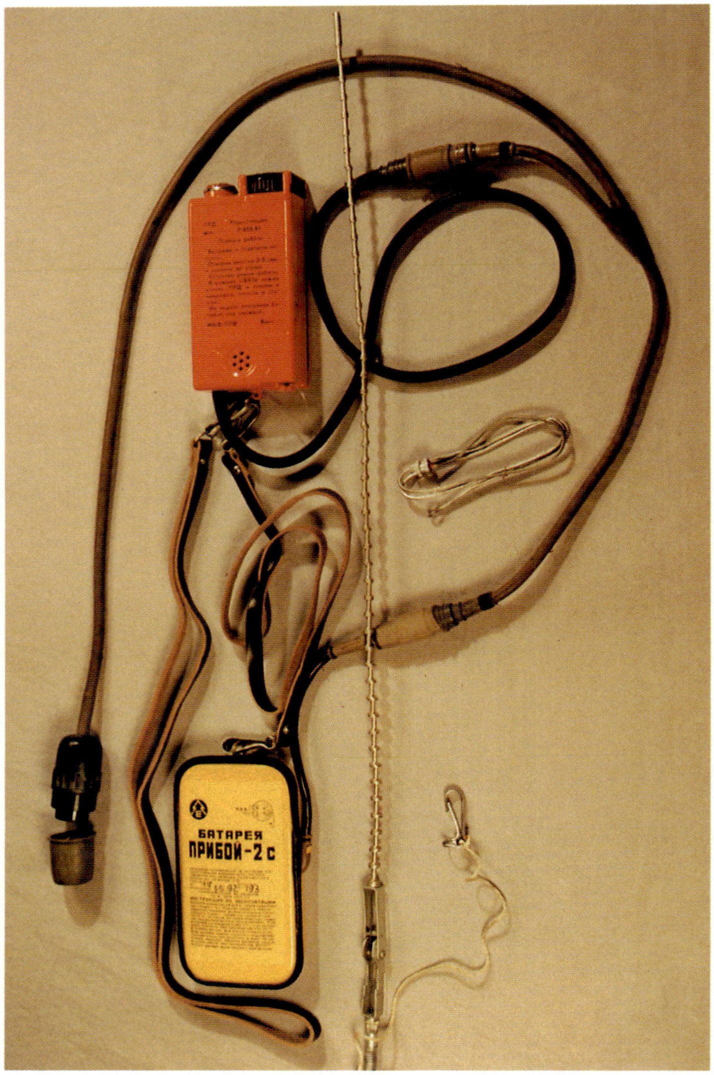

Using the same "Priboy-2S" battery as the R-855UM, it is also issued with either type antenna. Shown here is the R-855A1 with leather neck lanyard. Another leather strap connects the radio to the battery to protect connection cord. Shown also is the unique helmet/radio adapter.

The R-855A1 is a dual-band UHF-VHF radio with a choice of four functions: UHF 243.0 voice or beacon mode; VHF 121.5 voice or beacon mode. VHF 121.5 is the international civil aviation emergency channel.

The helmet/radio adapter allows the superior earphones and microphone of the various pilot helmets to be used with the radio. This also allows the radio to be monitored under extreme weather conditions which might otherwise be very uncomfortable. Shown in use with a ZSh-7M helmet with a KM-34D Series 2 mask.

Edged Tools

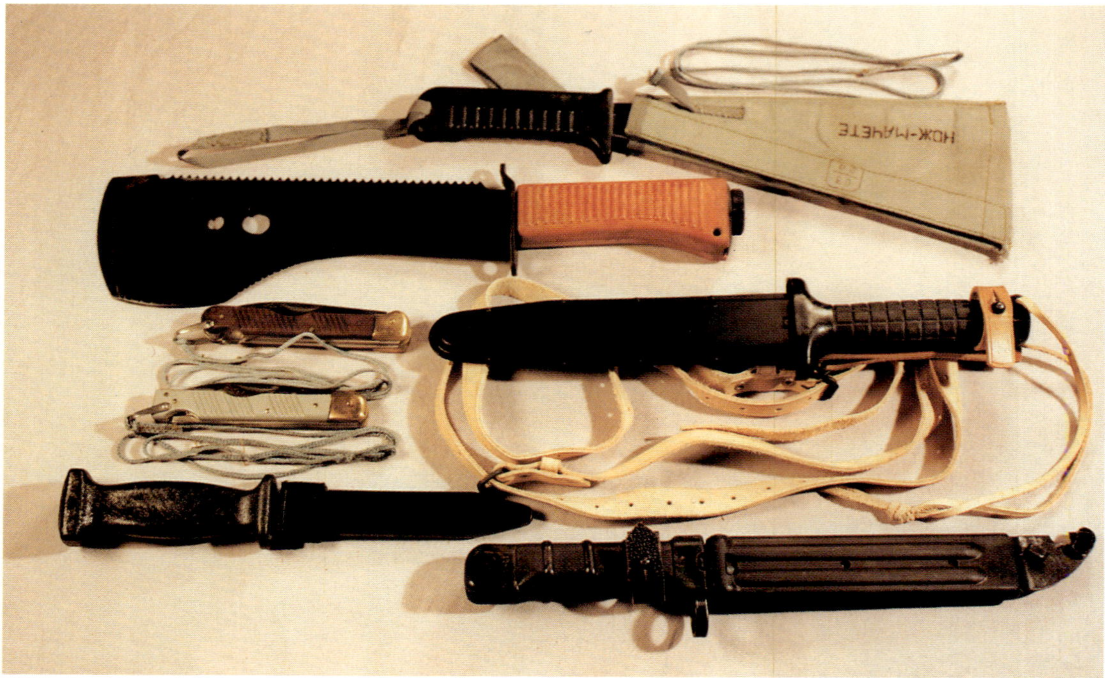

Several types of edged tools are used as implements of survival by a variety of aircrews. (top to bottom): Triangular knife-machete; survival multi-tool; folding lock-blade knives; Spetznaz commando knife; paratrooper knife; and AK-74 bayonet.

Early type knife-machete with two-part handle which much be assembled when needed. Two screws seen near blade secure handle. Blade is hard chromed.

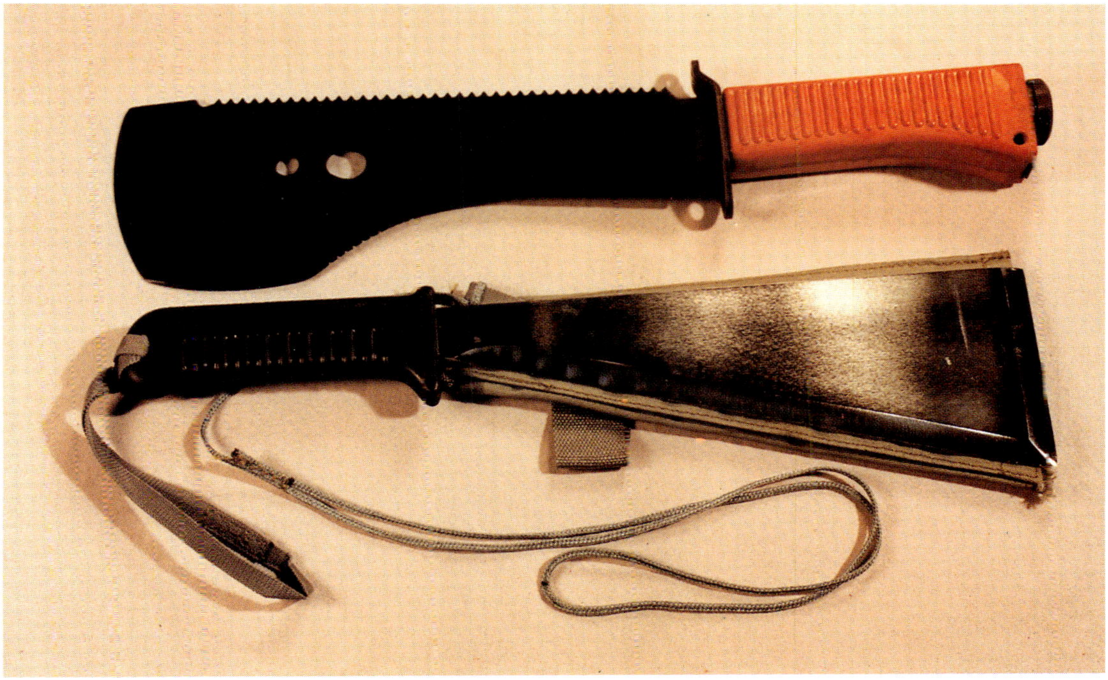

The current type knife-machete (bottom) is serial numbered and has a 235mm blade which is sharp at the end as well. It is a very practical design offering good balance with excellent chopping performance. Control is enhanced by a molded, no-slip handle. Side of blade is used for hammering, such as stakes. The survival multi-tool is a recent design (top) offering similar chopping ability with added features such as saw blade on top.

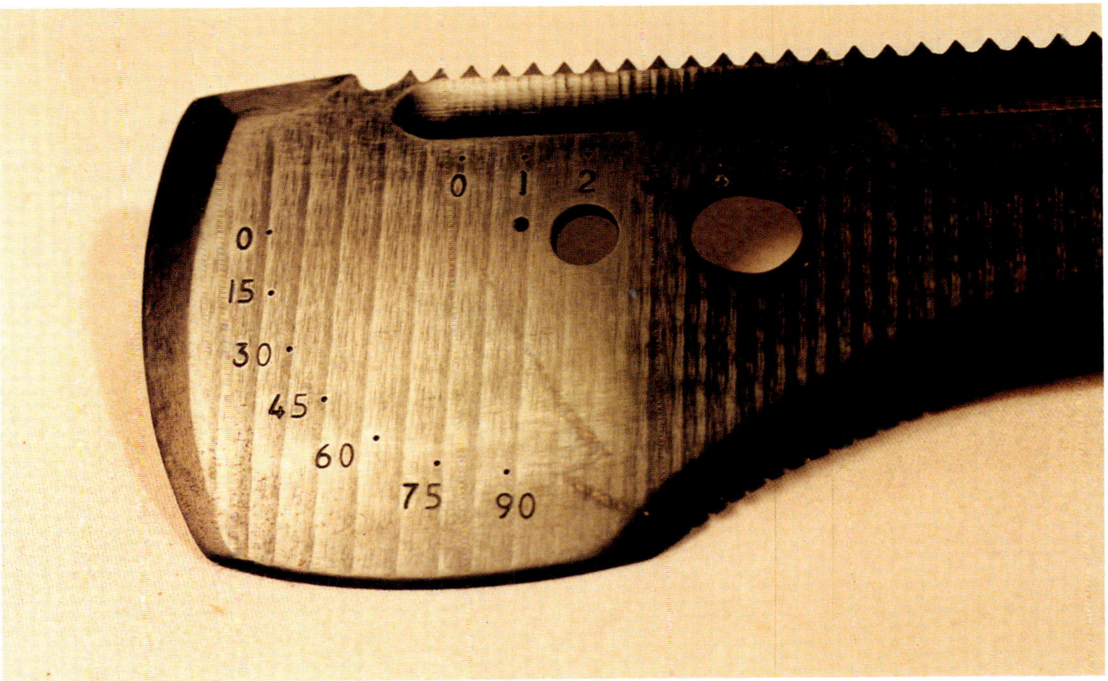

The black carbon-steel blade of the survival multi-tool has a sharp portion for chopping; a less sharp section for hammering; and the end is sharpened for scraping. A centimeter rule is along the top of the blade below the saw teeth and a protractor is also stamped in the side of the blade.

The orange handle is hollow, offering storage for small items and an ice pick (shown) is available by reversing the bracket at the end of the handle. The pick can also be used as a leather awe.

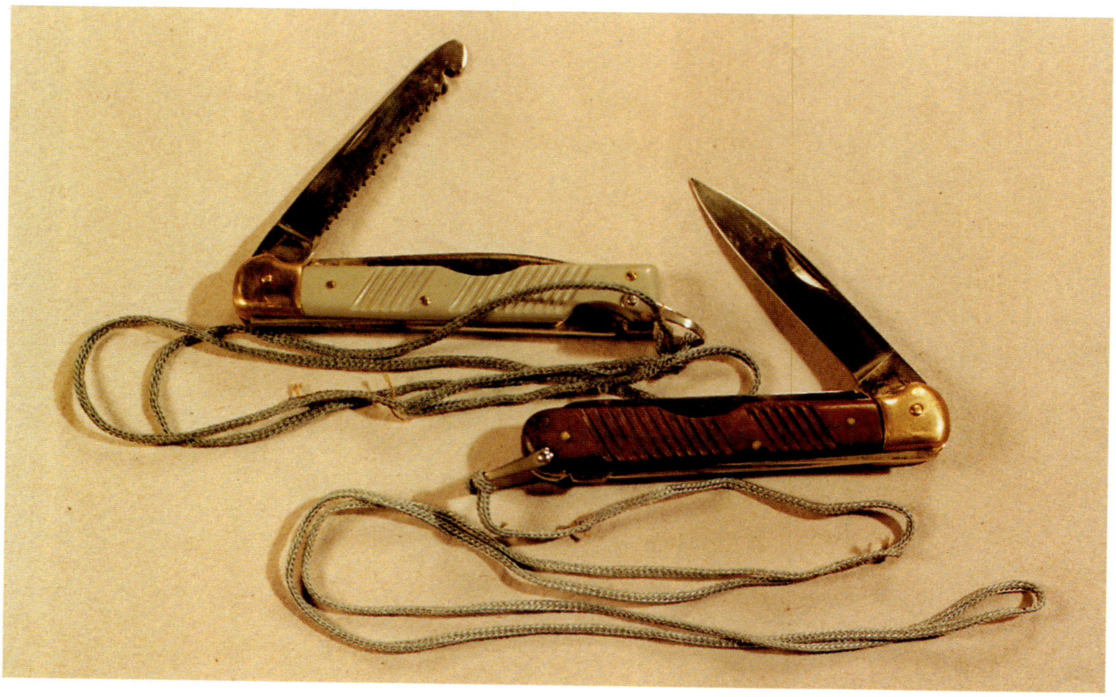

The folding knife has a locking knife blade and a saw/ screwdriver blade. The knives have no markings and are used in most kits.

The paratrooper knife is standard issue to airborne troops and is often used by pilots as well. It has two sharp blades; one serrated, one plain, and a simple plastic sheath. It is carried in the flightsuit.

The bloody war in Afghanistan prompted concerned aircrew to arm themselves with whatever weapons they could obtain. Pistols and assault rifles weren't enough. The first choice, but hard to obtain, is the Spetznaz commando knife (top). It offers a very strong and sharp blade designed for fighting. The other choice is the standard AK-74 rifle bayonet.

ABOVE AND RIGHT: The Spetsnaz knife has a thick blade with a saw tooth edge and a protective steel sheath. It is worn strapped to the right leg, ready for instant use.

The bayonet offers an effective wire cutter feature which was in use on Russian bayonets long before the U.S. M-9.

Selected Components

The Makarov is a very dependable semi-automatic pistol based on the German Walther PP. It is standard issue throughout the former Soviet Union both in the military and police. It has an 8 round magazine and uses a 9x18mm. round nose cartridge. Often carried by aircrew, it is supported by a 16 round aluminum ammunition box issued in many kits.

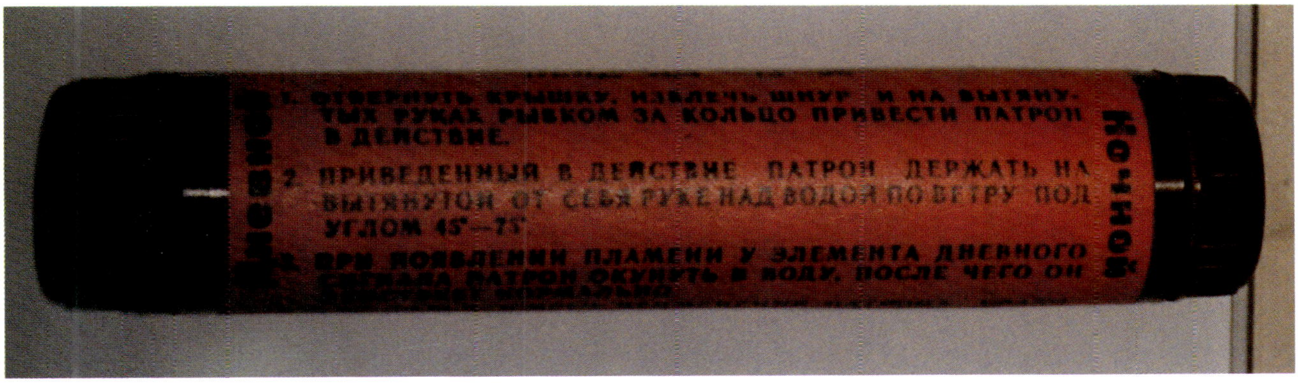

The PSND hand held flare offers 30 seconds of bright orange smoke from one end for day use, and 60 seconds of bright light from the other end for night use. Water tight caps seal each end and instructions (reprinted in Chapter 3) are printed on the side.

The MEM-76MI strobe light is individually serial numbered, waterproof, and floats. It is usually issued with one or two extra batteries and has a flash rate of approx. 60 per minute.

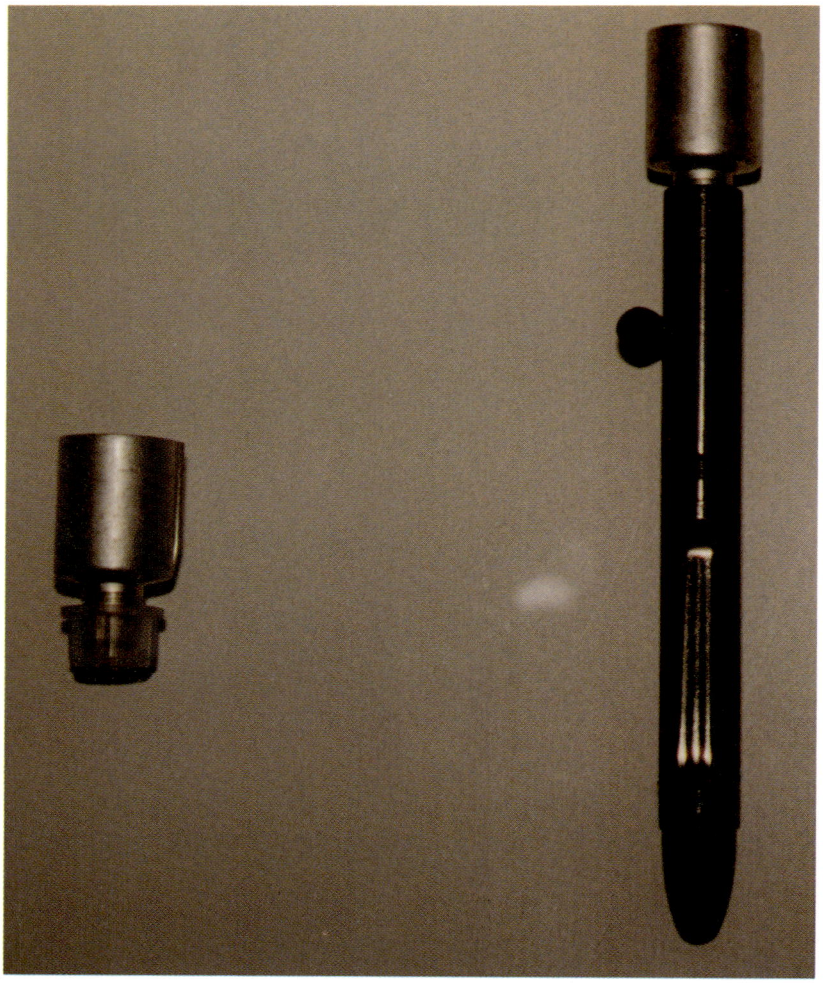

The standard issue 15mm. flare set is comprised of 15mm. flares which thread onto a hand held launcher. Flares use a primer and are offered in several different colors. Flares launch to an altitude of over 300 meters and can be seen for 25 kilometers.

The signal mirror is used in many kits and life preservers. It is all metal and, therefore, very rugged.

Instructions suggest, in short: "Opening mirror, and connecting reflected dot with hole to control direction of flash. Use only for emergencies; use occasionally even if no aircraft is spotted as flash can be seen for many kilometers."

CHAPTER 2
AIRCREW SURVIVAL TECHNIQUES

Russian aircrew survival training includes instruction in a number of subjects which are not covered in the survival manual. This is a common circumstance in most types of military training. This chapter covers several of these subjects based on their unique nature and to perhaps help fill-in-the-gaps in the manual reprinted in Chapter 3.

A Russian pilot or aircrew member is instructed that even under the most extreme and seemingly hopeless circumstance, one can survive using the most powerful tool he has: his mind. The training motto reads, "To give up in your mind is to die . . ."

Most survival training is carried out on a unit level and is supported in the classroom with posters depicting the various items in the survival kits. It is believed by seeing these posters almost daily, a pilot is reminded of the subject and its importance in his life.

FIELDCRAFT

The ability to boil water is important, whether for purification, cooking, or washing. If one is without a vessel in which to boil water over a fire, all is not lost. Here's how:

1. Dig a bowl shaped hole near your campfire.
2. If available, line the hole with any waterproof material such as fabric or plastic, or use clay. As a last step, line it with several layers of parachute material.
3. Fill with the clearest available water (see manual).
4. Locate several fist-sized rocks which are smooth, round and dry.
5. Heat the rocks in your campfire until they are extremely hot.
6. Using two sticks as tongs, place the rocks into the water.

An effective water purification filter can be constructed using a tripod made of sticks and parachute fabric fashioned into three layers:

1. The top layer should have 15-20 cm. of sand.
2. A layer of fabric.
3. 20-25cm. of charcoal.
4. A second layer of fabric.
5. 10 cm. of small gravel.
6. A third layer of fabric.

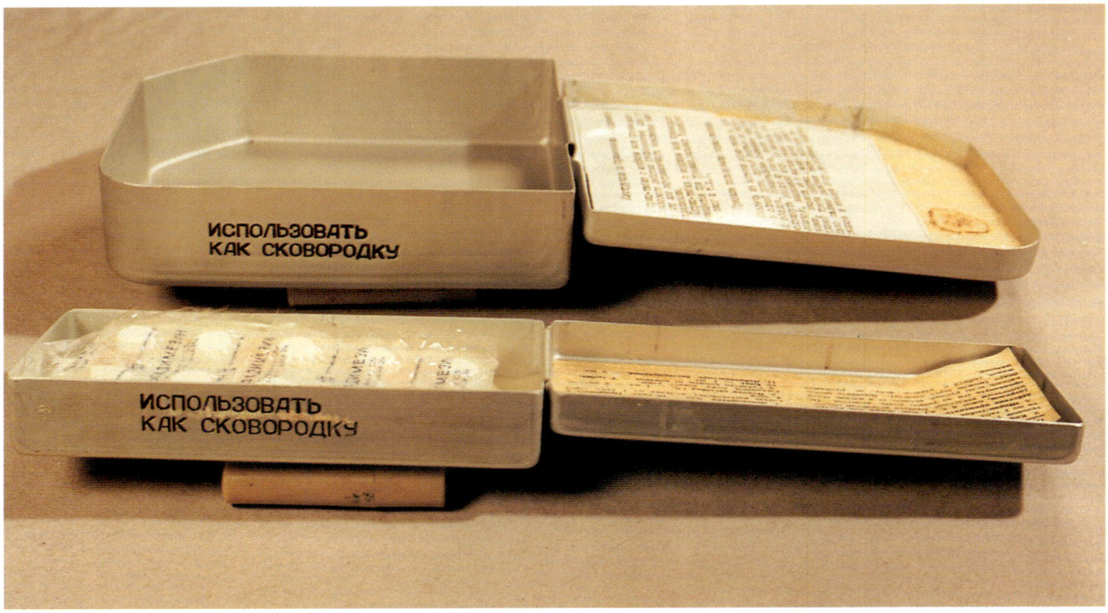

Some of the aluminum storage containers found in both the NAZ-7 and NAZ-7M are designed to be connected together with their lid to form a frying pan. In this manner, water or food can be heated over a campfire. (As instructed on the side of the container).

The ability to travel may be essential to survival. In this regard, some items are designed to be carried on the flightsuit belt ready for use such as the machete and water bag.

The flight map can be used as a survival map. Protect it by placing it in the plastic along with the survival instruction manual. Remember, the darker the color, the higher the elevation

DURING WAR TIME . . .

In a hostile environment, movement and camouflage are most important. If at all possible, hide yourself in daytime and only move at night. Use shadows and obstacles to hide yourself. Avoid roads, railroads, waterways, etc.

A camouflage flightsuit and survival hat helps to hide your presence. Note how bright the skin appears. Cover all exposed areas with mud. This can also act as an insect repellent, but without the odor which could give you away. Cover other reflective surfaces such as wrist compass.

The face netting on the survival hat hides the skin well and provides insect protection. But if moving, can be easily snagged and entangled on vegetation. Pistol should be used only as a very last resort. Remember: accuracy is limited to 25 M.

Retain your flight map only if no tactical or other secret markings exist on its surface. Do not add any markings such as friendly force locations, your direction, etc. Destroy by burning, or soaking in water, then mutilate.

CHAPTER 3

INSTRUCTION No. 1907-2670

PROCEDURES FOR AIRCREWS IN UNINHABITED/WILDERNESS AREAS AND ON THE SEA, FOLLOWING EMERGENCY LANDING OR AIRCRAFT EGRESS

1991

INSTRUCTION No.1907-2670

PROCEDURES FOR AIRCREWS IN UNINHABITED/WILDERNESS AREAS AND ON THE SEA, FOLLOWING EMERGENCY LANDING OR AIRCRAFT EGRESS

An emergency landing on the ground or on the water or by parachute after a plane crash can occur in a totally uninhabited area, very far from cities or villages.

If you suddenly find yourself in such conditions far from civilization, remember, that a happy ending is primarily dependent upon yourself, and from your knowledge of how to survive.

To survive- you must act very purposefully, to use your emergency equipment and natural materials cleverly and at the same time, to apply all of your knowledge and experience for protection from the influencing elements of high or low temperatures, wind, solar radiation, and for obtaining water and food, etc.

You should carefully size up the situation, and not panic. Try and remember everything you know about safety at the same time. Your actions should all be specific, and thoughtful, considering the type of location, distance from civilization and the health of the rest of your crew.

Your will, bravery, courage, logic and resourcefulness will make you successful even in the most extreme situation.

CREW PROCEDURES AFTER EMERGENCY LANDING IN A WILDERNESS AREA

After an emergency landing:
- immediately exit the aircraft;
- as soon as possible move the injured members of the crew to a safe location and provide first aid;
- if possible, remove and bring along all of the emergency equipment and parachutes;
- prepare to operate the emergency radio set, establish communication with any radio station which can hear your signal;
- organize a temporary base camp;
- assign responsibilities to all the members of your crew. Yet always take into account their abilities;
- orient yourself to the area and specify your location;
- prepare for immediate action all signal equipment in case of visual sightings;

If your aircraft was abandoned from the air, try to gather the crew. For this use voice signal, sometimes it is useful to shout or to use a whistle.

Usually the commander abandons an aircraft last, so other members of crew upon landing must locate the aircraft on their own. In these situations you should take into account the distance wind might carry your parachute.

- If you don't locate all of your crew members after regrouping, you should organize a search.
- If you don't know your location or the distance to any place where people live, it is better to remain in the same location without traveling. It makes your rescue more likely and you will have more time to protect yourself from the influences of the environment, to save your energy and to protect your health until help arrives.

You should leave the location of your landing only:
- if you know the exact location of your landing and the location of the closest city or village. And it is possible to overcome this distance; after taking into account the stamina and fitness of everyone.
- if you see a river, road, way or place of civilization when you were dropping in your parachute;
- in case of threat of your life; like a fire in the forest, a crack in the ice under or near your camp, a flood, etc.;
- if during 4-5 days you can't establish communication with any radio station, with a base or with a searching helicopter;
- in case of military actions, if you are on the side of your rival;

OPERATION OF SIGNALS AND SIGNAL DEVICES

There are different devices for signaling; by radio, a supply of visual sighting devices: signal cartridges; rockets; signal mirror; packs of dye; remove these from the NAZ (Emergency Escape Kit) after landing.

Radio Operation. Connect the battery to the radio and check it. In severe cold weather, keep the battery under your clothing. The complete emergency signal system includes a VHF-UHF short-wave radio type R-8551M ("Priboy-2S") with an effective range of 25-100 Km, depending upon how high the search airplane (helicopter) is flying.

You should follow these rules to establish contact:
- Attempt contact immediately after landing and for 10-12 min. duration, and at the beginning of every hour for the first 24 hours from the location of the crash or landing. You should send a signal: "We have crashed!", give your call-sign and coordinates. After every attempt to make contact, wait 3 minutes. The rest of the time, the radio should be on receive;
- During the next 24 hours, at the beginning of every hour make a triple broadcast about the emergency. After that make a broadcast every 5 min., then turn it off;
- In case of contact with an airplane or helicopter, or in case of visual sighting, establish a two-way connection, after broadcasting a new signal about the disaster. In case of uncertainty, try to use hand signals switching back after 1.5-2 min.;
- If you establish a two-way connection with an emergency searching aircraft, you must act as they command you.

If you have an automatic radio beacon "Komar-2M" immediately after landing check the condition of the radio by listening, for this bring the unit to your ear. These automatic radio beacons can broadcast only signals of emergency. It can work for 24 hours and it has an effective range of 25-100 km. to reach search airplanes (helicopters).

If you contact a searching helicopter, switch to radio type R-855UM "S."

You must follow the next order when you work with ALRAM (SW) radio for general use:
- Unfold radio antenna, broadcast the message three times consistently in telegraph and in voice modes, after every message switch on receiver for 3 minutes; First day after the crash, repeat broadcast signals for 10-12 min.

"SOS" 24 times; approximately once per hour, but the rest of the time place on receive;
- Next day repeat, but just 3 times a day to conserve the battery;
- At the beginning of every hour set automatic broadcast signals "SOS" for 5 min., then receive signals for 5 min., then turn off the unit.

Operate in the beacon (SW) radio mode, on frequency 8.364 Mhz. (R-851) or 8.929 Mhz. (R-850). Change to another frequency only after special instructions.

Broadcasting about the crash has to be next:
- Radio-voice signal "SOS" - 3 times;
- Combination "GE"- 1 time;
- Beacon- 2 times;
- Latitude- 2 times;
- Longitude- 2 times;
- the word "receive"- 1 time.

Use of Visual Signals. You should use visual signals only when you see a search aircraft (helicopter). In daytime, signal by the "day end" of the signal device, PSND. When this is burning, it produces bright orange smoke for 30 seconds. The "night end" of the PSND burns a bright red color, which can be spotted from a long distance. Every PSND signal has directions written on its side. When you use the signal, the wind should blow to your back, and you should hold the device in an outstretched hand. When using a signal device, operate in a clearing, otherwise the smoke or glow will disperse between the trees and no one will see it.

Another effective signal device is the special signal mirror, but only in sunny weather (Picture 1).

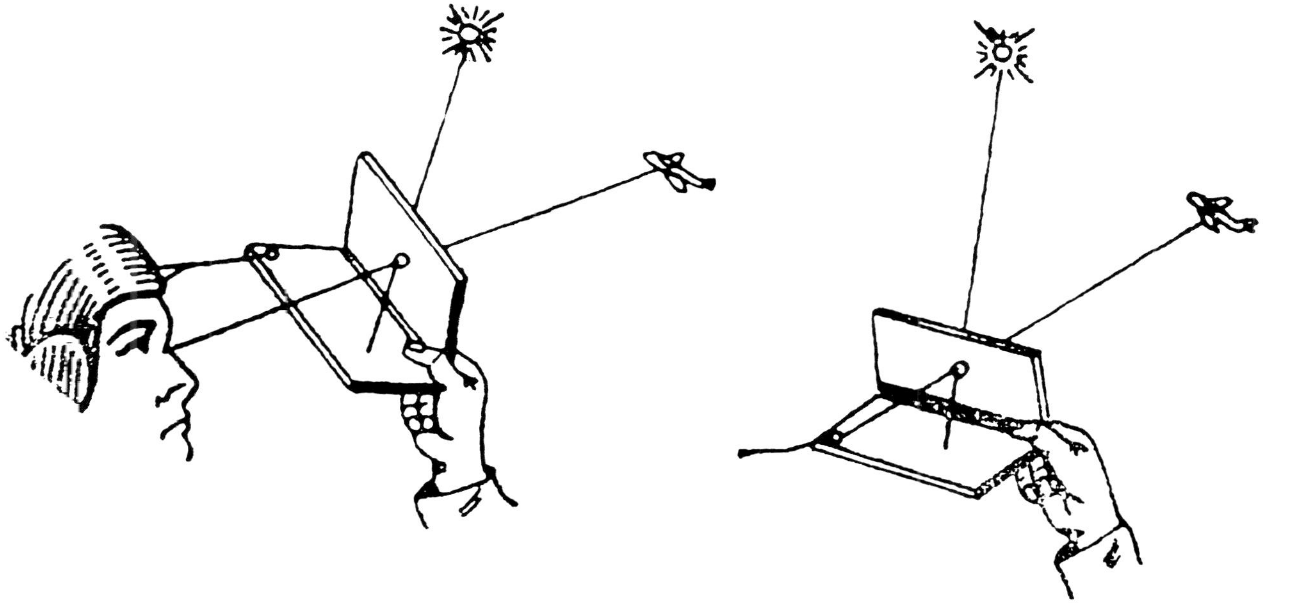

10-5876

Picture 1. SIGNALLING WITH THE MIRROR

Periodically, pass the signal mirror along the horizon. Sometimes search aircraft can see you much sooner than you can see or hear them.

Another good method of signaling is the common campfire. In daytime you can place on the fire fresh grass and leaves in order to produce thick smoke. Black smoke can be produced with the help of tires or engine oil. Prepare a camp fire in advance on a hill or any other open place. In winter, cover a prepared campfire with a piece of parachute fabric or fir tree branches in order to protect it from snow. It is better to burn a camp fire continuously if there is enough fuel.

Construct a parachute canopy signal (picture 2). Tie the large sections of parachute fabric to the tops of high trees or stretch the canopy out as identification: or place the canopy over the bed of a small creek. If you have landed in the forest and the parachute canopy has hung in a tree, do not remove it because it is beautifully seen from above.

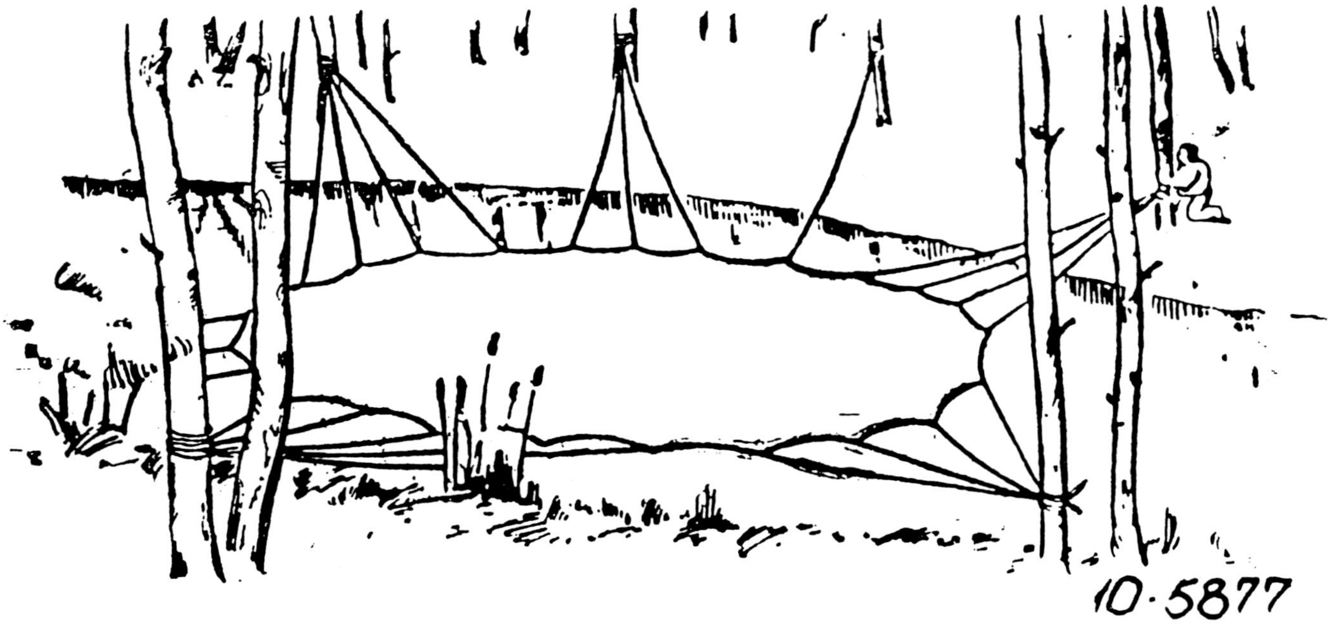

Picture 2. USING YOUR PARACHUTE CANOPY AS A SIGNAL DEVICE

If you land in the Arctic, periodically remove the snow from the fuselage in order for it to be better seen from the air.

If a search aircraft appears, use the dye marker as a signal. Make a wide stripe in the snow with the powder. A bright stain of orange color is easily seen from a long distance. Use no more than half of the package at one time. Make several signal campfires if you have enough fuel. It is possible to burn dead trees directly when they are standing timber.

You can report about the health of your crew and necessary help to the search plane/helicopter using the International System of "Ground-Air" Visual Signals which is illustrated on pages 9-10.

INSTRUCTIONS

HOW TO USE 15mm SIGNAL CARTRIDGES

1. Unscrew and remove the protective cap from the cartridge.
2. Place the bottom of the firing handle in the upper slot of the device and screw in the cartridge firmly as far as it will go into the threads.
3. Before firing, place the bottom of the firing handle in the lower slot in the device.
4. Holding the device firmly with the cartridge in your out-stretched hand (angle of 80-90 degrees) fire by slipping the handle to the left side with your thumb. In order for the cartridge to fire, do not allow the handle to slow down when released.

NEVER:

1. Put your hand over the end of the cartridge while screwing into device.
2. Aim the cartridge of the loaded device at yourself, people, buildings, and other areas.
3. Operate within 100 meters of highly flammable materials.

FINDING YOUR BEARINGS USING CARDINAL POINTS

After completing the emergency procedures, try to determine your location using the last data about the route and duration of your flight, landing time or the time from when you abandoned your airplane. Remember special landmarks that you have noticed during the flight and the decent in your parachute. If the route map is saved, mark on it the approximate landing area. Having established a connection with a search plane or any radio station, report your data immediately.

If you do not have a compass, it is possible to find cardinal points using the sun, stars, or local landmarks.

International System of "Ground-Air" Signals

Signal Definition	Signal	Signal Definition	Signal
Medical emergency-serious casualties	I	Will try to take off in plane	I >
Medical kit needed	I I	Aircraft is badly damaged	L⅂
We cannot move	X	Landing will be save here	△
Food and water needed	F	Fuel and oil needed	L
Weapons and amunition needed	⩔⩔	Everything is OK	LL
Map and compass needed	□	No	N
Radio needed	¦	Yes	Y
Indicate direction to move	K	Do not understand	JL
I am moving in this direction	↑	Mechanic needed	W

Finding your bearing with the sun. In the northern hemisphere you can find the north direction at noon by standing with your back to the sun. Your shadow will point to the north, the west will be to your left side, the east to your right side. In the southern hemisphere the north will be behind you, the east to the left, the west to the right.

Local noon can be determined by using a vertical pole with a length of 0.5-1.0 meter; vertical alignment of the pole is checked with a plumb made of parachute line and a tied stone. (Picture 3)

Before high noon approaches, mark with a peg the end of the shadow and continue to make marks when the shadow begins to grow longer again. The moment when the shadow is the shortest and corresponds to the passing of the sun over the present meridian, i.e. to the local noon.

Finding your bearing with a watch. Place your watch horizontal and turn it until the big hand points towards the sun. Draw mentally the line across the center of the watch face and the digit 1 (direction A). The bisector of the angle between this line and the big hand shows north-south direction; notice that the south is to the right from the sun before noon and it is to the left afternoon (Picture 4)

Finding your bearing with the stars. In the northern hemisphere the north direction can be found with the pole star which is situated approximately over the north pole. Locate in the sky the Great Bear Constellation which has a typical shape of a scoop with a grip. Draw mentally a straight line from one end star to the other. Continue mentally this line and mark on it five

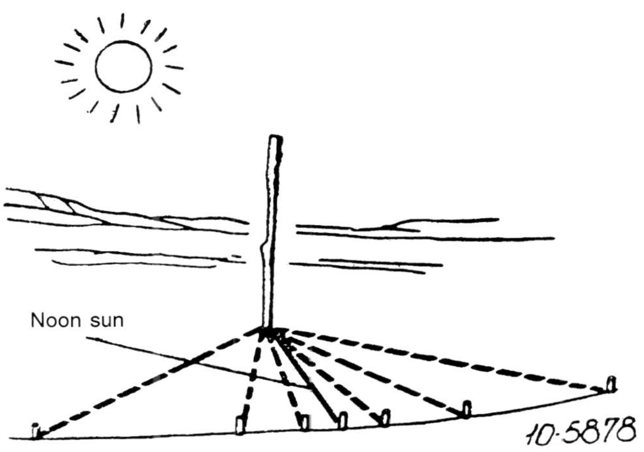

Picture 3. METHOD OF FINDING LOCAL NOON

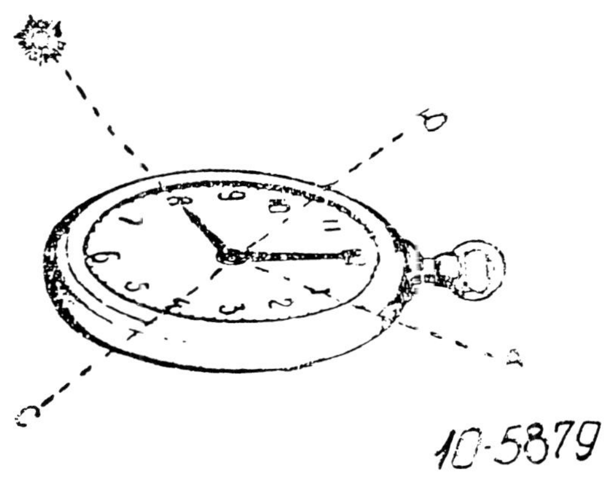

Picture 4. FINDING THE CARDINAL POINTS WITH A WATCH

(5) times the distance between two end stars. A bright star will be found on the end of the fifth segment, this star is called the Pole Star. The direction to the Pole Star corresponds to the northern direction. (Picture 5)

In the southern hemisphere the cardinal points can be found by the Southern Cross Constellation which includes four stars situated as a cross. Mentally draw a line which goes along the long axis of this constellation which is directed to the north. Do not confuse the right Southern Cross and the wrong one including five stars that are less bright and further from the other.

Finding your bearing using local landmarks. In the Taiga (Siberian forest) the cardinal points can be approximately established by certain natural signs. For example, wood bark is rougher on the northern side of the tree. Birch or pine bark is darker on the northern side. Trees, stones, rocks are covered more with lichens and mosses on their north side. If the thaw has set in, the snow stays longer on the northern slopes of the hills. The ant-hills are usually better protected with trees, bushes, stones from the north. The mushrooms usually grow next to the northern side of the trees. The coniferous trees discharge more sap drops to their southern side. These signs are especially noticeably when the trees are situated farther apart from each other and grow separately. In the spring grass grows faster on the southern slopes and many blooming bushes have more flowers there.

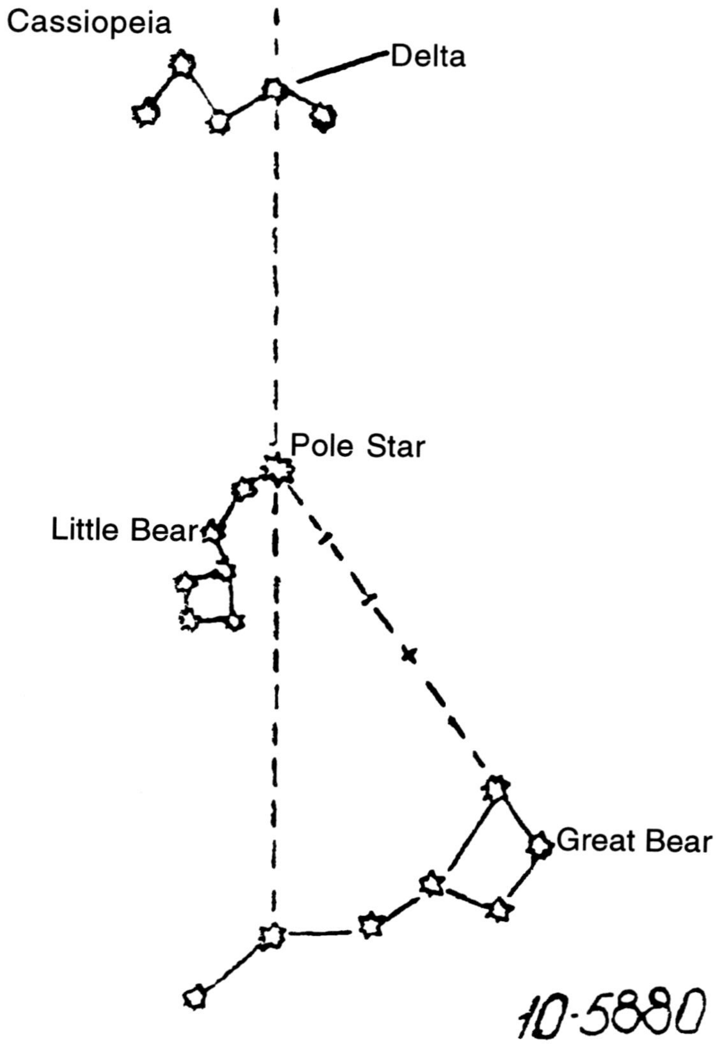

Picture 5. FINDING CARDINAL POINTS USING THE STARS

TEMPORARY SHELTERS

There are a lot of different kinds of shelters: lean-tos, tents, snow houses, trenches, tee pees, etc.

The choice of your shelter will depend on your conditions. You can use materials which you have available. You can also use the fuselage of your aircraft as a temporary shelter.

You have to conserve your energy. Don't build a large shelter on the first day. You will have a time for that later.

It is easy to make a simple roof or hammock- with half of a parachute in the summer in the forest (pic. 6).

In cold weather, it's better to make a shelter like (pic. 7,8,9 and 10).

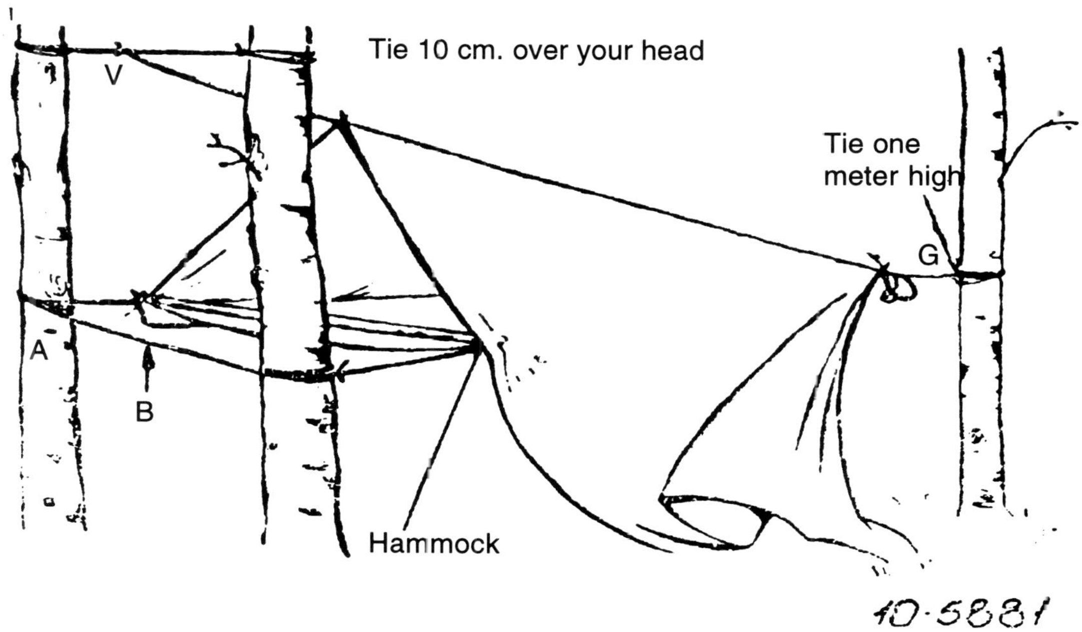

Picture 6. HOW TO CONSTRUCT A SHELTER USING PARACHUTE MATERIAL TIE BETWEEN TREES TWO SHROUDS 1 METER ON THE HIGH SIDE; AND THEN TIE ONE UNDER THE ANGLE TO ANOTHER (VG). TIE ONE END OF THE PARACHUTE TO THE SHROUD (AG). STRETCH THE FABRIC AND TIE IT TO THE (BT) SIDE. AND THROW THE FREE END OVER THE (BG) SHROUD.

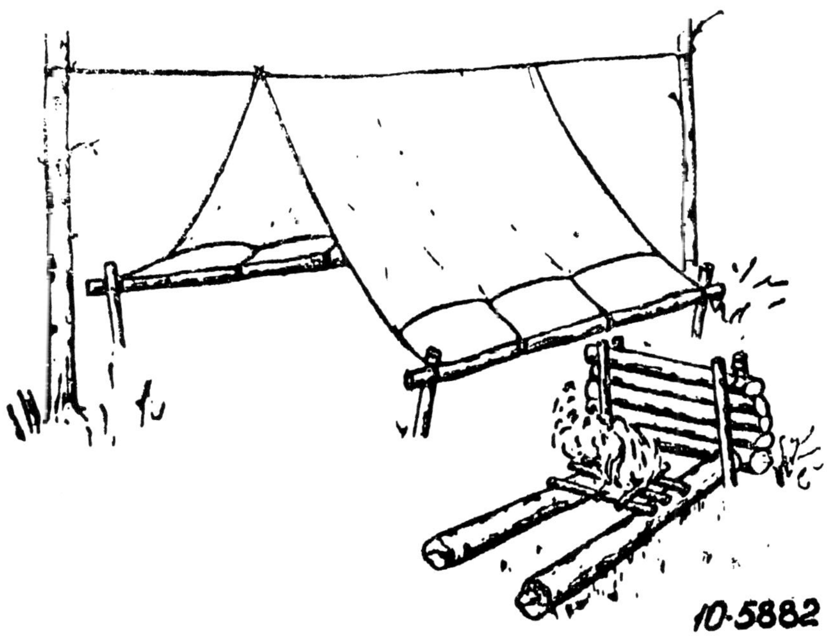

Picture 7. HOW TO MAKE A TWO-SIDED SHELTER USING PARACHUTE FABRIC STRETCH ONE SHROUD LINE BETWEEN TWO TREES. THROW THE PARACHUTE FABRIC OVER THIS SHROUD LINE AND TIE THE ENDS WITH THE HELP OF ADDITIONAL SHROUD LINES TO THE POLES.

Remove snow from a place chosen for construction then dry the soil by using a camp fire for 1.5-2 hours.

It is recommended to cover your shelter with branches and parachute in the time of rainy weather. When it's dry and cold weather- you must set the parachute under a hut of branches. It's recommended to cover a floor by branches, grass and use parachute fabric, even better, use a lifeboat and life vest.

CONSTRUCTION OF SHELTER IN THE ARCTIC AREA

You must chose a place for construction which is protected from wind with deep (at least 1 meter) snow coverage. To dig a hole or lair or to build a dwelling use the following recommendations:

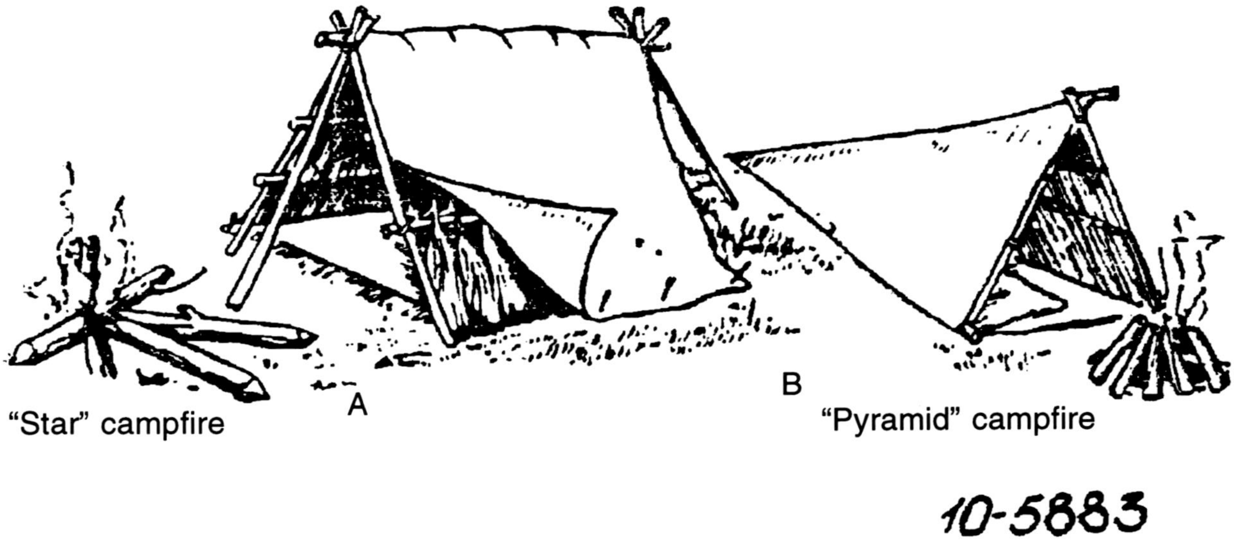

Picture 8. HOW TO CONSTRUCT A SHELTER OF BRANCHES: A-BIND TWO SUPPORTS. USE THREE POLES (1.5-2 METERS) TO MAKE THE SUPPORT STRONG. THEN CONNECT IT WITH DIAMETRICAL POLES. AND COVER THE STRUCTURE'S FRAME WITH BRANCHES. MAKE THE TOP OF PARACHUTE FABRIC; B-MAKE THE FRAME STRUCTURE FROM FIVE POLES. THE FRAME STRUCTURE SHOULD HAVE A SHAPE AS ILLUSTRATED IN PICTURE 9, PAGE 11. THEN COVER THE FRAME WITH PARACHUTE FABRIC AND FROM THE OPEN SIDES STAKE TO THE GROUND. USE A SHARP TENT STAKE WHICH CAN BE PRODUCED WITH PIECES OF BRANCHES AND STICKS. LOCATE THE ENTRANCE ON THE LEAST WINDY SIDE.

Picture 9. CONSTRUCTION OF A ONE-SIDED SHELTER

Picture 10. CONSTRUCTION OF A TWO-SIDED SHELTER. LOCATE TWO DIAMETRICALLY GROWING TREES. MAKE A FRAME OF BRANCHES (1.5-2 METERS) AS SHOWN IN PICTURE 10. AND COVER IT WITH BRANCHES AND LEAVES. START AT THE BOTTOM SO EVERY LEVEL CAN BE COVERED BY THE NEXT AT LEAST BY HALF.

SNOW TRENCHES. In a snow hill with a depth of 1-1.5 meters deep, dig a trench. It should have a width which would be enough for one or two people. Place the bottom of the inflatable rubber raft up. Inflate it firmly and place it on the floor. Make a roof from parachute fabric and fasten it with blocks of ice or snow. (Pic 11.)

WIND BREAK. If the snow isn't very deep, you should construct blocks (Not too large) and build a wall from them- like a protective wall- with a height of 1.5-2.0 meters. The sizes of every block should be -10x40x70 cm.

Build the wall perpendicularly to the usual direction of the wind. Pack in several layers of parachute fabric. And leave one side on the top of the snow wall and fix it with snow blocks. (Press the fabric down). With another piece of fabric, heap up with piles of snow and ice.

SNOW CAVERN. The most comfortable shelter is the snow cavern (Pic.12). Into a snow hill with the height of 1.5-2.0 meters dig a tunnel. Then make it wider at the end. It should be wide enough for all members of the crew yet you should consider the thickness of the snow. Make a space large enough to lay down and rest. This space must be a level higher than the floor (40-50cm). Remove extra snow from the cavern. Inflate the rubber raft firmly and turn it bottom up and use it as a mattress. At the top of the cavern, carefully breach a hole for ventilation. At the entrance to the cavern heap snow or hang a piece of fabric.

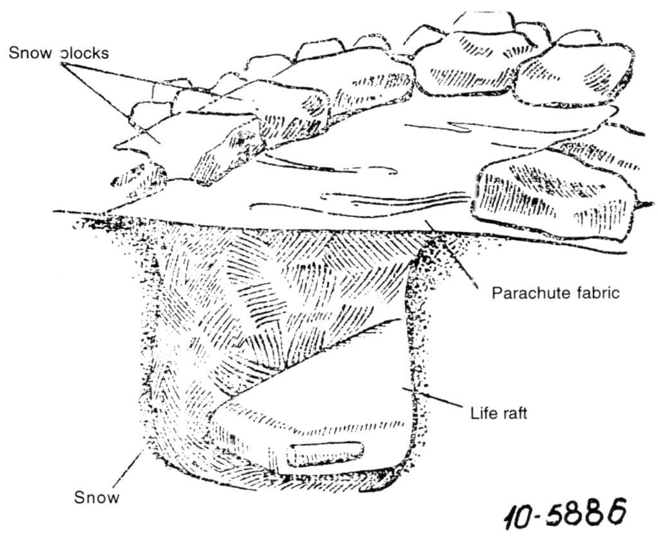

Picture 11. CONSTRUCTION OF A SNOW TRENCH

SNOW HOUSE (IGLOO). The most reliable building under arctic conditions is the snow house or "Igloo" (Pic. 13.) This kind of building was used by Eskimo people.

It is the best protection from wind, low temperatures and it is rather roomy. In order to build this shelter, look for a place with deep and compactable snow. With help of a shroud line and a knife, draw a round groove which will be the diameter of the shelter. Choose the diameter of the future shelter taking into account this rule: for 1 person- 2.4 meters, for 2 persons- 2.7 meters, for 3- 3 meters, for 4- 3.6 meters for 5- 3.9 meters.

Clear the surface for the shelter. Then level an area for preparing snow blocks from the down wind side of the circle. The trench which will be formed by the preparation of snow blocks will be the entrance to your shelter (igloo). With the help of your knife or folding snowshoe from the NAZ kit, cut snow blocks with a length of 50-90cm. and a width of 40-50cm. and a height of 10-20cm. For removing blocks from the trench you should cut from every side of every block at least 3-5cm. and then plunge the knife or ski into the crack under the block and carefully, with even pressure, break it loose a little bit. After this you will be able to remove block after block. When you have made 10-15 blocks, start to stack walls on the perimeter of the sketched circle.

Before installing each block you should cut one side of each one lower so that it has an inside slope of igloo 15-20 degrees. Through the first row make a spiral cut.

Into the flute, which was the place where the first block of the second row is set, butt-end and compact the block to the last block of lower row. For building the next levels, cut blocks inside the shelter and adjust them using the height rule. Some little blocks should remain inside for building snow benches. Every next level must be inclined inside at a greater angle than the lower row. The last few blocks of the shelter should stack almost horizontally. For the final block in the dome there should be just a small hole - and the edges of the blocks should be cut to an angle of 15 degrees from the vertical. (Pic.14.)

The outside size of the hole has to be greater than the inside but made oblong in order to pass it through the dome. When you are finished with the walls, you should fill the chinks with snow. Cut a hole in the wall above the trench in order to make an entrance.

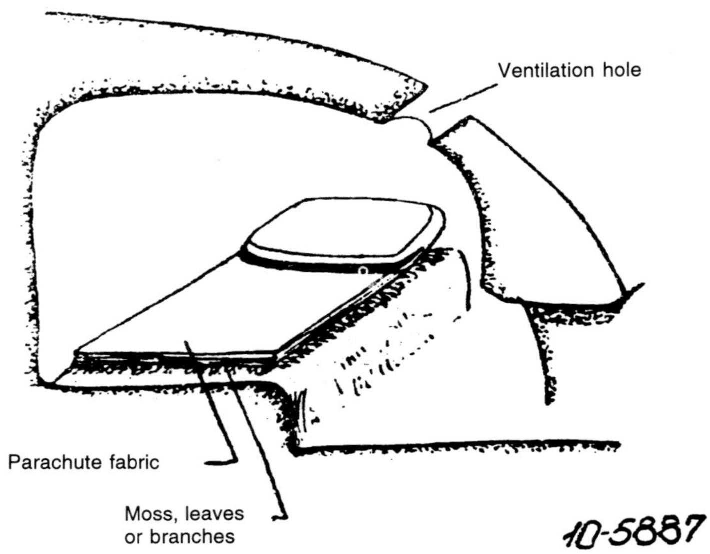

Picture 12. THE SNOW CAVERN

Opposite the door you can make a bed at least 50-70 cm. in height and cover it with parachute fabric or use an inflatable raft. Make a table of snow blocks. Don't forget to make a ventilation hole, then set a fire and prepare a hot beverage.

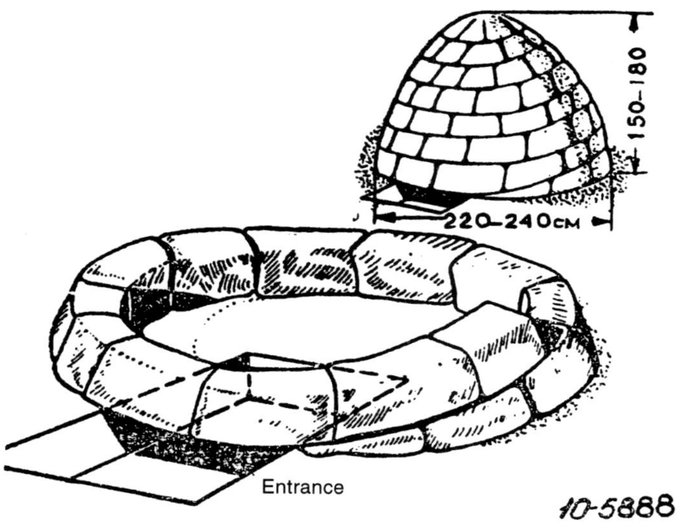

Picture 13. CONSTRUCTION OF A SNOW "IGLOO." FIRST DIG A SNOW TRENCH 10-20cm DEEP, 50-90cm LONG, AND 40-50cm WIDE FOR AN ENTRANCE. THEN LAY OUT A CIRCLE 110-120cm. CONSTRUCT SNOW BLOCKS AND LAY THEM IN A SPIRAL PATTERN AS ILLUSTRATED.

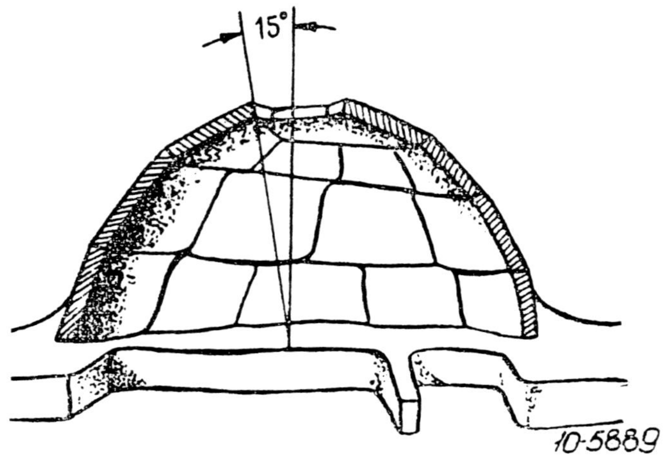

Picture 14. CONSTRUCTION OF THE VENTILATION HOLE

CONSTRUCTION OF SHELTER IN THE DESERT

If you can not find a natural shelter, simple sun protection can be constructed from your parachute canopy. Spread the canopy on the sand and fold it in two or three layers. Use parachute shroud lines to stretch the canopy. Cut the lines where they are fastened to the straps of the riser system, then fasten the free ends of the straps to a plant stalk. The root system of desert plants is so extensive that these plants can hold up the canopy even in strong winds

If you can not find any plants- you can fix it taunt with the help of a sandbag anchor made from a piece of parachute fabric, size 0.5 x 0.5 meters filled with sand. Tie the free ends of the shroud and the anchor, then dig into the soil a depth of 40-60cm. Six to eight anchors are enough to set up an awning. Inflate your life-raft, and put it under the center of the awning, installing it side way's (pic 15).

You can also form a central pillar with the help of your NAZ kit's storage container. Fill it with sand and tie it in place with shroud lines. You can create additional space by digging out the sand from under the awning if it is hanging too low. Don't dig in the area around the pillar; remove the sand around this area very carefully.

You can make another type of simple shelter by digging a hole in the sand a depth of 1.5 meters and covering it with three layers of parachute fabric. Then fasten the material around the border with the help of stones and sand.

CAMP FIRE PREPARATION

After building a shelter, build a camp fire. A campfire is heat, a hot meal, and dry clothes And an important means of signaling.

Try to store up plenty of firewood if you are able to do so. Select a place for your campfire away from the wind. In winter, flatten the snow or make a base from wood when the snow is very deep.

INSTALL PARACHUTE ENDS WITH SHROUDS, TIE IT TO THE TREES, PLANTS, OR USE SAND ANCHORS.

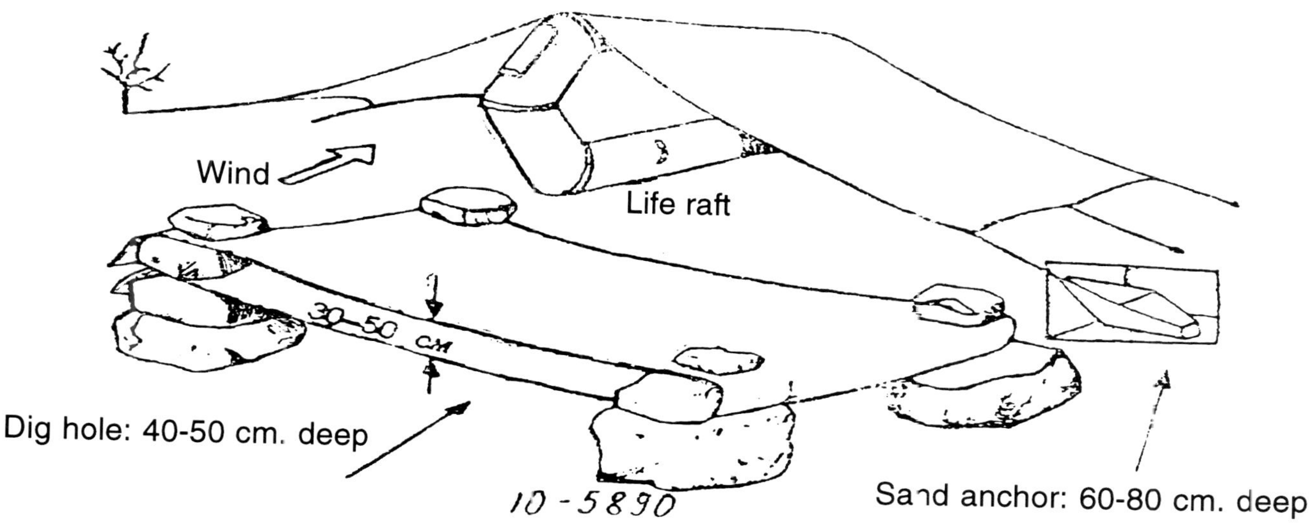

Picture 15. CONSTRUCTION OF SHELTER USING YOUR PARACHUTE AND LIFERAFT

Never build a campfire under large trees in the winter because the snow on the branches will fall and put out the fire. And in the summer you should not set a fire next to a big dry pine tree or in the underbrush, dry grass, or dry moss. It can cause a major fire. Don't leave a campfire without attention. Take a smoldering coal and put the rest out with water when you leave the camp. Make in advance a base of sand, ground, or soil when you are preparing a fire on the surface of a dry swamp or peatbog. Otherwise the fire can spread into the peat soil and this can also cause a major fire. And don't make too large of a campfire, it can cause a forest fire. Gather in advance a few dry branches for making a fire; prepare by whittling them, but leaving the shavings still on one end of every branch. Surround them with dry moss, birch bark, and little branches without leaves. In rainy weather use the fire-starters from your NAZ kit. Put into the fire additional firewood very carefully so you don't put out the fire.

Be conservative with matches. Your supply is limited.

Be very careful when you use gasoline or other combustible liquids on a campfire. Never pour them directly onto the fire.

If you have enough firewood, you can make a fire as shown on picture 7-10.

In the arctic regions useful combustible materials are wood, which has been cast ashore by waves, drawfish trees, peat turf, dry grass, and fat from seal or polar bear. It is recommended to cut the peat turf into small pieces and to dry it if possible. The dry grass is better tied into straw so it will burn longer.

Aircraft fluids can be useful as a combustible material if you have survived an emergency landing. Immediately drain the oil before it thickens in the engine. Thicken it on the snow, if you have the resources.

Make a fat lamp for heating your dwelling. Empty out the box from the NAZ kit's first-aid box and fill with pieces of seal or bear fat. Make two or three wicks from cotton fabric or bandage material. Then rub it with fat. One lamp of this type can provide you enough light and heat to raise the temperature inside your shelter above freezing.

In places such as desert and steppe in winter time it is possible to improvise metal stoves, which can be made from gasoline or oil cans, or with parts from your aircraft. Fuel can be rags and seat covers doused with kerosene, oil, or gasoline, or pieces of rubber and other easily-burned materials.

Select a place for the campfire so the sparks can't hit inside your shelter. Don't forget to provide good ventilation, if you build inside the shelter a fireplace or a fat lamp. Otherwise you'll run risks of poisoning by carbon monoxide. It is possible to start a fire without matches or lighter with the help of flint and steel. For steel you can use a scrap of steel or your knife's blade, knife's butt or hard stone. Strike sparks from the flint as close as possible to the tinder, so that the sparks hit on it.

Blow on the smoldering tinder very carefully before it flames up.

It is easy to make tinder from dry crust, cotton wool, bandages, moss, or even bird feathers. Douse the tinder with a few drops of gasoline or add to it a little bit of gunpowder.

You can also start a fire with the help of a lens from a camera, or eyeglass, or you can make a lens yourself. Stack two watch lens together. Do it with the bulge sides out. Fill up the space between them with water and seal it with clay around the borders.

Concentrate the rays on paper or tinder. Or you can create a fire with a night signal flare.

RENDERING EMERGENCY FIRST-AID AFTER LANDING

Act immediately. Use bandages from the first-aid kit and other clean materials from NAZ.

INSTRUCTIONS TO STOP BLEEDING

In trauma situations with severe damage to blood vessels-first stop the bleeding. Press directly on the wound with the aid of a bandage. Apply a sterile dressing with a small roll of gauze and tie it tightly. If the injury is to a large vessel- for emergency bleeding control- press with your thumb on the artery tightly against bone at one of the pressure points, which are illustrated in picture 16.

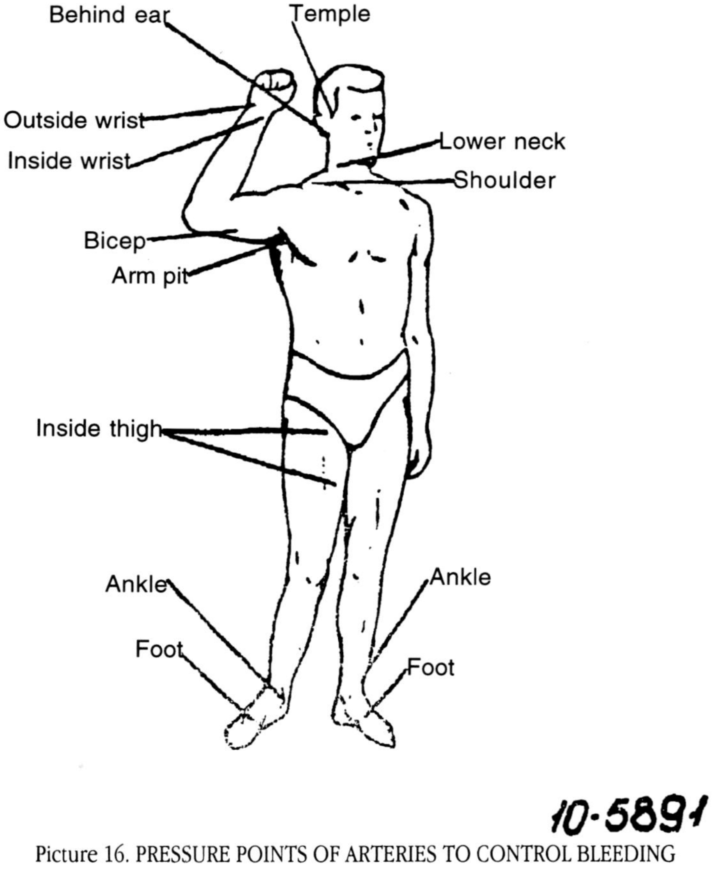

Picture 16. PRESSURE POINTS OF ARTERIES TO CONTROL BLEEDING

In cases of injury of the artery in the shoulder, press to the bone the shoulder artery on the inward side of the two neck muscles. Press the thigh's artery to the thigh bone inside the thigh.

Press to the jugular inward in cases of face or neck injuries. (Picture 17.)

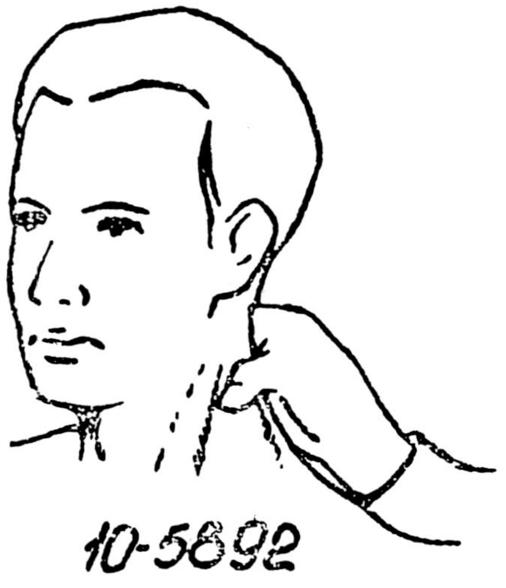

Picture 17. STOPPING THE BLEEDING FROM THE SLEEP ARTERY

Press on the under-neck cavity and at the same time press chest artery to the first rib. (Picture 18)

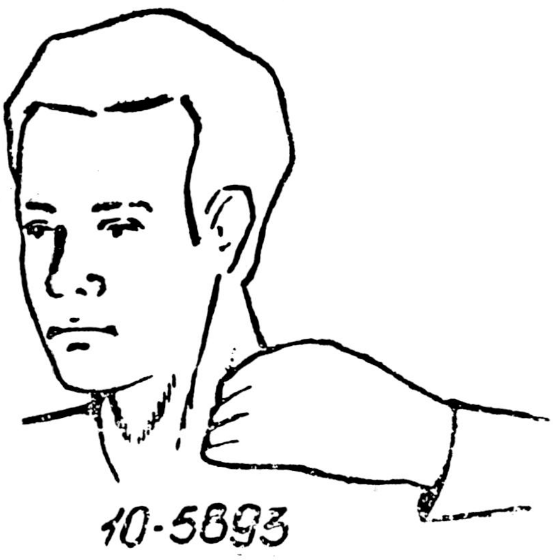

Picture 18. STOPPING THE BLEEDING FROM THE CHEST ARTERY

You can stop severe bleeding of an extremity with a tourniquet (Picture 19).

A strong strip of clothe or bandage is the most convenient method to stop the bleeding of an extremity. Tie it around the leg or arm above the wound then tighten it forcefully by twisting with something stiff until the bleeding stops. Fix the ends of the tool. Use a fabric strip made from a piece of parachute if you don't have anything else. (Picture 20)

Don't tie the strip directly to the body. Lay a piece of bandage or parachute fabric under it.

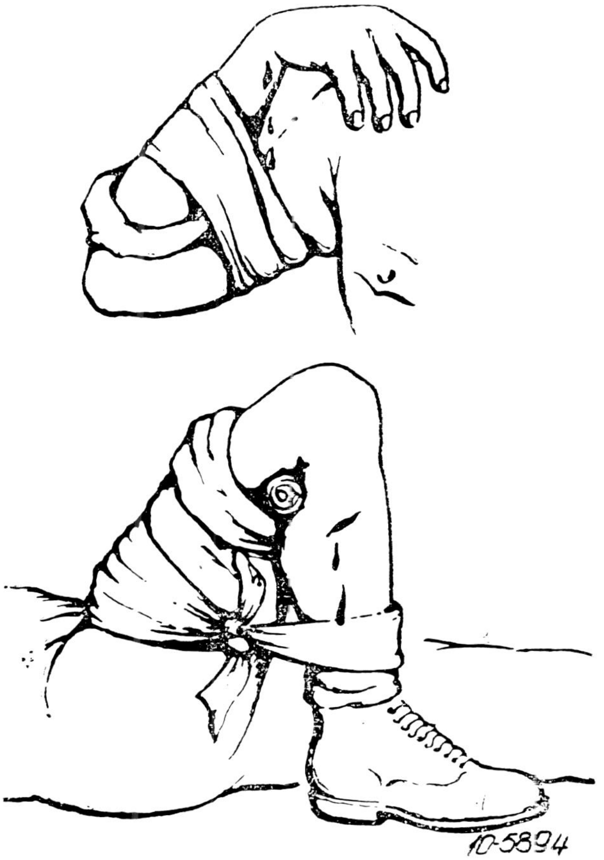

Picture 19. THE STOPPING OF BLEEDING BY BENDING THE EXTREMITY

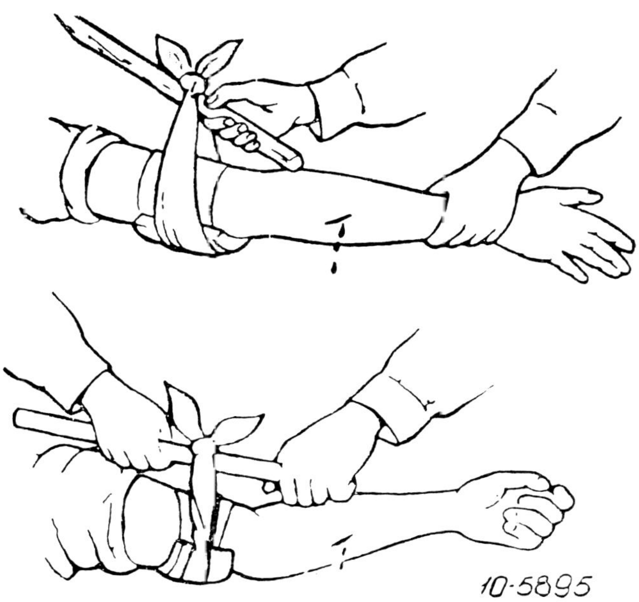

Picture 20. USING A TWIST TOURNIQUET

Don't keep the tourniquet on longer than 1.5 hours because complete restriction of blood flow can cause tissue damage. By the end of (1.5 hour) this time press the bleeding vessel with your finger and loosen the tourniquet for a few minutes to refresh the blood circulation of the wounded extremity- it will get warm and pink.

Apply the tourniquet above or below the previous location if it doesn't stop bleeding.

You can stop a nose bleed if you put cotton wool balls or gauze into the nostrils. Sit down the wounded person and throw back his head a little bit. Place on the nose a bandage soaked with cool water, a roll with ice or snow on the nose and the forehead.

PROCEDURES FOR FRACTURES

FRACTURE OF AN EXTREMITY. Symptoms: strong pain, swelling, change in shape of the extremity and the failure of it to function.

Lay the injured person down immediately on the ground, calm him, give him a pain relieving medicine (as analgin or promedol). Secure the injured extremity, guaranteeing it's immobility.

The most reliable method of stabilizing a broken extremity- is the splint. You can construct one from branches, bunches of reeds and other handy materials. (Picture 21)

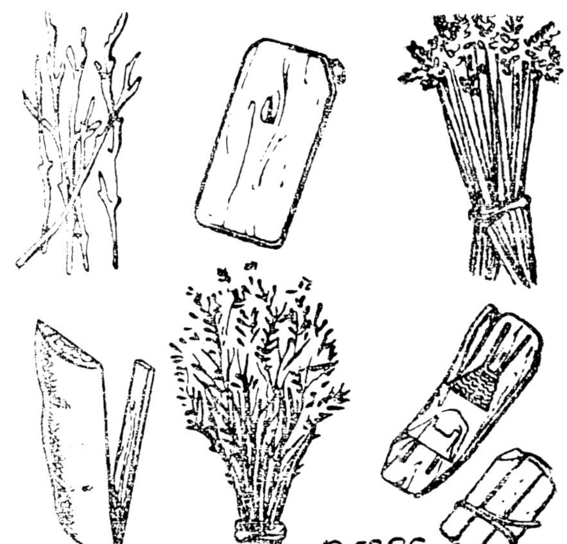

Picture 21. HANDY SUBSTITUTE MATERIALS FOR CONSTRUCTING A SPLINT

REMEMBER THESE RULES WHEN USING A SPLINT:

-the splint must reach beyond the joints above and below the fracture, in case of fracture of the thigh -all the joints of the extremity (Picture 22):

-don't place a splint directly on the skin.

-clean and wash the wound, apply iodine around and put a sterile bandage on, before splint installation.

If you don't have any handy materials in case of a fracture of the shoulder, you can simply bandage the arm to the body. Don't forget to place a roll of grass or parachute fabric under the armpit before bandaging. Bend the arm at the elbow joint to an angle of 90 degrees and turn the hand palmside to the body (Picture 23).

You can bandage a broken leg to the healthy one.

FRACTURE OF THE RIBS. Symptoms: Severe pain, which is made worse when breathing in or out, and coughing.

Place a tight bandage around the chest and use pain relieving medicine.

FRACTURE OF THE SPINAL COLUMN AND PELVIS. Symptoms: In case of fracture in the neck area of the spine with injuries to the spine: main symptom is the lose of sensation and the ability to move (paralysis).

The main symptom of a hip bone fracture is an inability to stand up or to sit down, and even to raise a leg or to turn the body from side to side in a laying condition.

Lay the victim on a flat surface. Give pain relieving medicine. You can move the victim from place to place only on a flat board.

INTERNAL HEAD INJURY. Symptoms: Bleeding from the nose, mouth, ears, and unconscious condition.

Secure rest for the victim. Put sterile bandages on the open cuts.

DISLOCATIONS. Symptoms: Great pain in the joint and the inability to move the joint; visual change in joint shape in comparison with similar/opposite extremity. Secure extremity from moving with the help of a bandage and splint.

BRUISES OR STRAINED LIGAMENTS. Symptoms: Severe pain, swelling in the location of the injury.

Apply a tight bandage.

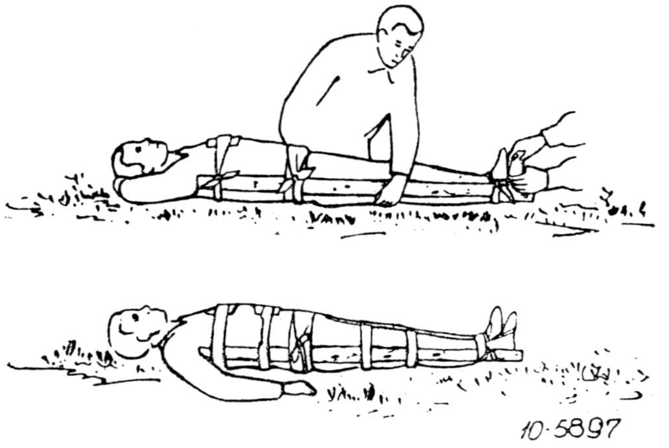

Picture 22. HOW TO SPLINT A LEG

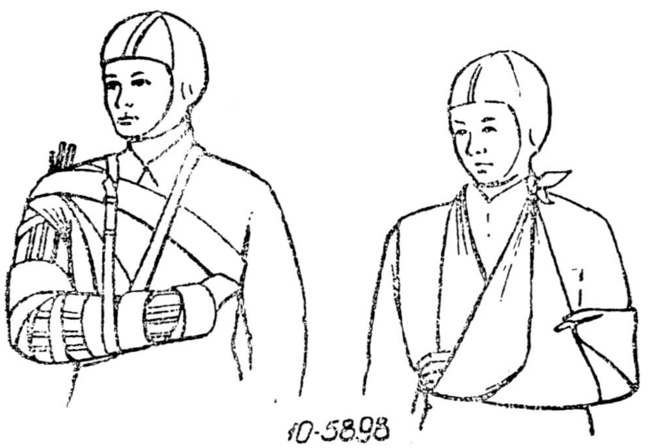

Picture 23. HOW TO SPLINT AN ARM

TREATMENT OF BURNS

Burns can be divided into three categories:

- First degree- skin is red and swollen;
- Second degree- blistering;
- Third degree- numbness of skin and deep tissue burns (damage)

First of all take the burnt clothing off. Apply a sterile bandage, or use a band-aid. Don't open any blisters that appear. This can cause infection. Give a pain reliever to the victim if the area burnt is large. It is important to give to the victim a lot of liquids to drink (tea, water, coffee, etc.)

TREATMENT OF FROSTBITE

Symptoms: skin becoming white, the lose of sensitivity. Rub the frozen places gently with gloves, fur from a hat, etc., until sensation returns.

Never rub with snow. Ice crystals can easily injure damaged skin and it makes pain worse and can cause infection.

Carefully cut and remove the shoe from the foot, if it was frozen. You can warm frostbit arms and legs by using warm water before the blood circulation is restored and then apply a sterile bandage. Warm the victim and give him plenty of hot drinks.

TREATMENT FOR STOPPED BREATHING

In this situation lay the victim on his back, clean his mouth and nose of any blood, mucus, then loosen his belt, pants, collar, and start immediately men-made breathing.

In the case of drowning, first of all, remove all mess, slim, from the mouth and nose of the victim. Then, stand up on one knee and lay victim on your hip so that his body is hanging down. Remember the victim must lay on you hip so that his stomach is down and his back is up. Then press on his back with one hand and use the other to hold his legs. Relieve the airway from water and then immediately begin man-made breathing.

INSTRUCTION FOR MAN-MADE BREATHING (MOUTH TO MOUTH METHOD)

Tilt victim's head back all the way. For that place your right hand under the victim's lower head. To maintain this position, place a fabric roll under his shoulders. Then, keeping one hand on the victim's forehead to keep it rotated back, press the other on his chin, keeping his mouth open. Breathe deeply into the victim's mouth, do it so that you mouth fully covers the mouth of the victim. And then make him breathe out. (Picture 24)

Picture 24. ARTIFICIAL BREATHING (MOUTH TO MOUTH METHOD)

When his chest has expanded, stop breathing into his mouth. Let him exhale himself. Repeat 12-14 times per minute. Alternate the man-made breathing with indirect heart massage in cases of no pulse. For that, put one hand on the center of the lower part of the chest and press firmly. Make four strong compressions after every breathing segment. Make compressions very fast with an interval of one second. After breathing resumes, it is crucial to warm the victim by any means possible. Place a bottle with warm water or heating stones on the victim's stomach or legs. You should do man-made breathing until he breathes on his own or until obvious symptoms of death occur.

TREATMENT FOR UNCONSCIOUSNESS

Symptoms- loss of consciousness with sudden paling of the face, an appearance of cold sweat on the arms and face.

Lay the victim down immediately so that his head is lower than the rest of his body. Unbutton his collar and unfasten his belt. Give him a dose of liquid ammonia under his nose. Place a heating pad near his legs. After getting better, give the victim warm drinks.

TREATMENT FOR POISONOUS GAS EXPOSURE

Symptoms: headaches, sleepiness, giddiness, palpitation, nausea

Immediately get the victim to fresh air, give drinks of strong coffee or tea. Give man-made breathing in case his breathing has stopped.

TREATMENT OF SERIOUS STOMACH PROBLEMS

Symptoms: Pains in the stomach, nausea, diarrhea.

Don't eat for 24 hours. Drink 1-2 liters of warm water. Take 'levomicetin": 1 tablet per 4 hours until the symptoms disappear.

MEDICAL TREATMENT IN ARCTIC CONDITIONS

BECOMING TOO COLD - Do everything to prevent your body from becoming too cold. Remember that wet clothes lose their ability to keep you warm. Take off some clothes and unbutton your clothing to prevent excessive sweat resulting from hard work (building of shelter, carrying heavy weights). When pain or numbness appears in any extremity from cold, restore heat by increased activity.

SNOW BLINDNESS - an unusual burning on the eye's surface which is caused by the sun's ultraviolet rays, reflected by the snow. Symptoms: Sandy feeling under the eyelids, watery eyes, temporary loss of vision, pain.

Dark fabric, used as a bandage on the eyes and cold compresses help, in this case in 2-3 days. It is easy to protect your eyes with the help of sun glasses.

POLAR BEAR LIVER POISON - The liver of the polar bear contains a poisonous substance. In a few hours after eating, it can cause severe headache, stomach ache, nausea, and fever. Everything will disappear after 2 or 3 days, and a skin rash will disappear in 7 to 10 days.

Don't eat polar bear liver even if you are very hungry!

TRIXIHOZ (STOMACH WORMS) - Polar bear meat can sometimes have a special kind of stomach worm – trixins. To avoid infection-thoroughly cook all the meat or boil it before eating.

MEDICAL TREATMENT IN THE TAIGA

To protect yourself from any kind of gnats or mosquitoes use the anti-insect paste from your NAZ kit on all open parts of your body (arms, legs, neck, etc.)

You can spread a thin coating of the lotion on your skin. It offers good protection from all biting bugs.

To make the bugs disappear from your shelter, place smoldering coals in a metal can, metal box, or a piece of wood and cover it up with moss. Let the shelter become smoky and then let the fresh air in, help it by waving a piece of fabric or your clothes. Smoke can be placed near your entrance on the downwind side so that the smoke repels the bugs but doesn't travel inside your shelter.

TO AVOID TICKS- they are carriers of dangerous diseases. Not less than twice a day inspect all of your clothing and open areas of your body. Don't tear off ticks! It is better to cover it with iodine or to burn it with a cigarette or other hot item. Afterwards it will fall off by itself. Apply iodine to the wound. Remove the head with the help of a needle or pin, which has been sterilized with fire.

MEDICAL TREATMENT IN THE MOUNTAINS

Mountain disease - the most common ailment experienced in the mountains. The cause of it is rarefied air. Extreme effort, injury, and overstress- can all cause the development of this ailment. Symptoms: increased tiredness, shortness of breath, loss of memory, headaches, nose bleeds, nausea.

Build a rest camp and have a good rest, and a good hot meal in case these symptoms appear.

Take headache relief medicine from the first-aid kit in your NAZ kit.

Don't continue mountain climbing if you feel poorly.

To protect your skin from the sun's rays apply the sun block spray or cream from your first-aid kit from your NAZ kit or use a gauze bandage to protect your face. To avoid snow-blindness, use sunglasses.

Remember that the mountains can be a place of calm weather conditions or of great turmoil.

Organize and manage the mutual control and health of your crew members.

MEDICAL TREATMENT IN THE DESERT

The most dangerous influences of the desert are the sun's rays and the high temperatures. During the daytime try to stay in the shade, and limit hard work. Keep your clothing on, even in the shade. Loosen only your belt, and collar. Don't lay directly on the sand. In case of limited water supply, drink only what is necessary, and don't drink more than 50-70 grams, rinsing your mouth, before swallowing.

HEAT STROKE - the sick condition which is caused by excess heat in the environment. Heat stroke usually develops during the hottest part of the day. A mild case can be identified by headache and nausea. The pulse and breathing are rapid, pupils are dilated but the temperature of the body remains normal.

In more serious cases, heat stroke develops suddenly. And at first it appears that the victim has an extreme nervous system problem: delirium, hallucinations, oblivion. The breathing becomes quick and shallow. The pulse rises to 120-140 beats per minute. The face is red then pale with blue stains. The skin is dry and hot. The temperature of the body increases to 41-42 degrees.

Aid must be given immediately. Lay the victim in a shady location and remove his shirt. Spray him with water, wrap his face and body with wet rags, and rub briskly with a clothe or with your jacket. Rub the whole body briskly.

SUN STROKE - the sick condition, which is caused directly by the heat of the sun on the head. The first symptom is a headache, then weakness, giddiness, vision frustration, ringing in the ears, and nausea. The body temperature can rise to 39-40 degrees. Then it can increase to 40-42 degrees. Unconsciousness is a benefit.

For help – move the victim to a shady location and cool the body by all means possible.

DANGEROUS ANIMALS - In the desert you can often encounter poisonous snakes (Picture 25).

Be careful, don't step on the snake. Snakes often lay on cliffs between stones and in the rocks. In case of meeting a snake, don't move. Let the snake crawl away. Don't follow or pursue it. If the snake becomes aggressive, don't waste time, Hit it hard on the head, then finish it off.

In case of snake bite, make an incision in the location of the bite to a depth of 5-7 mm. If you don't have any cracks on your lips or cuts inside of your mouth, draw off the poisoned blood and spit it out. Wash the wounds and apply a sterile bandage. Immobilize the extremity with the help of a splint the same as with a fracture. And give plenty of liquids to the victim, (tea, coffee, water). In the desert you can encounter a lot of poisonous snakes, spiders and scorpions. To avoid spiders and scorpions, shake out your shoes before wearing them. Shake your clothes if you found a spider in them. Act as described above in case of spider or scorpion bite.

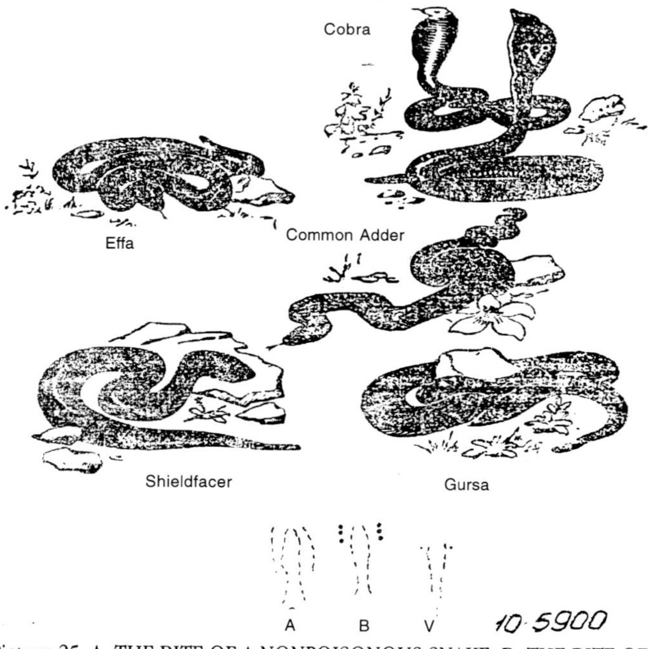

Picture 25. A- THE BITE OF A NONPOISONOUS SNAKE; B- THE BITE OF POISONOUS SNAKE; C- THE BITE OF AN ADDER

LOCATING FOOD AND WATER

To preserve human life and health, food is less important than water and protective clothing. Use the NAZ food supply very conservatively. Divide it to last 5-6 days.

Try to supplement your food supply with natural sources. Locations near the sea, the forest, and rivers are usually the best places to find natural food. Use all of your knowledge in hunting, fishing, and in the selection of edible plants.

HUNTING

The choice of prey depends upon your knowledge and supplies. Be very patient and persistent to be successful.

First of all find animal trails, watering holes, or eating places. Set up an ambush, using good camouflage. Set your ambush from down wind so as not to betray your position by smell or noise.

Sneak very carefully, only during a time when the animal is drinking or eating or looking the other way, if the distance between you and it is too great.

THE BEST TIME FOR HUNTING - is dawn (or early morning) or at sunset. Look for game near water and on the edges of a forest.

A lot of animals live in holes or burrows. To know if the animal is in the hole, you can use a stick. Put it in the hole and try to feel it. Sometimes you can take out the small animal (such as a lemming) with the help of a long branch which splits into two ends. Roll it inside the hole until it catches on the animal's fur. **NEVER EAT A SICK OR WEAK ANIMAL!** Usually, they carry disease.

SNARES, AND TRAPS - Use any strings or cords for preparing nooses. Different kinds of nooses and traps are shown on page 37 (picture 26) and page 38 (picture 27). Place the nooses on animal paths. You can easily find these trails, if you see fresh tracks or animal droppings.

FISHING

Fishing is the most reliable and easiest way to obtain food. There is a fishing kit and other fishing supplies in the NAZ emergency kit. It is possible to make fishing equipment with the help of other handy materials, if you are in short supplies from your NAZ kit. You can make fishing-line with the help of fabric strips or cords, and fish hooks from wire, a pin, or other metal: To tie hooks to the line, see pictures 28 and 29.

You can use worms, flies, or food remnants as bait. Also you can make bait with the help of aluminum foil, leather pieces, colorful fabric, plastic, or shiny metal parts.

Avoid walking on thin ice in winter (Cold) time.

Remember that places with dark clear ice are less dangerous, than places with snow cover.

Tie one end of a 20-25 meter long cord to a tree on the bank and the other to yourself before walking on the ice.

You can eat the meat of reptiles (as turtles, snakes, frogs) It is good to fry it before eating.

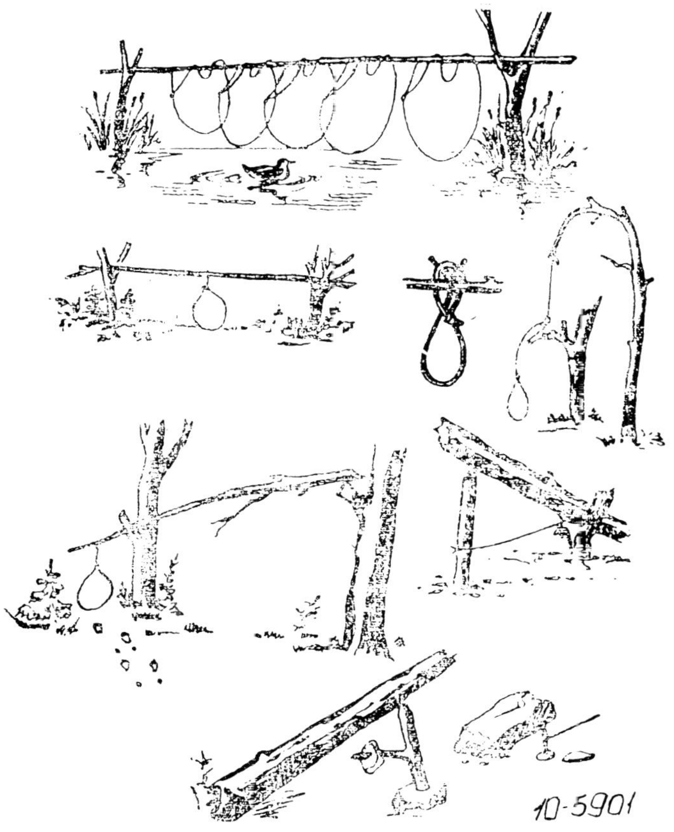

Picture 26. HOW TO CONSTRUCT NOOSES, SNARES, AND TRAPS

Picture 27. THE EASIEST NOOSE

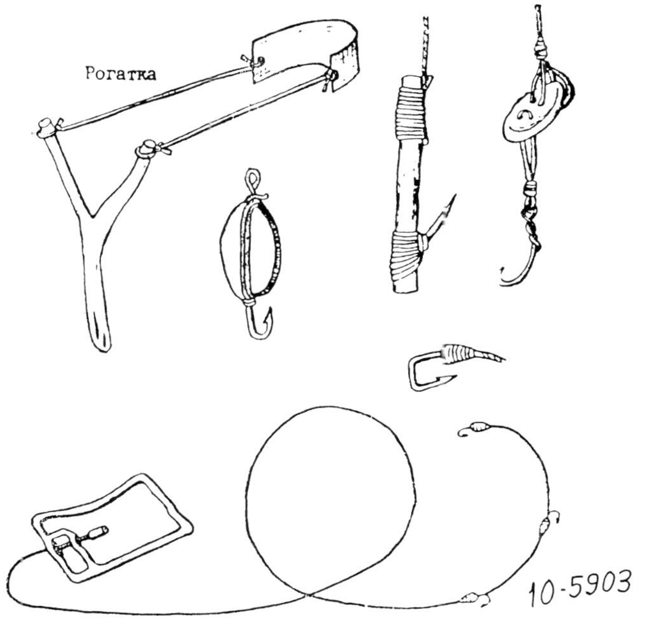

Picture 28. FISHING EQUIPMENT CONSTRUCTED FROM AIRCRAFT AND NATURAL MATERIALS

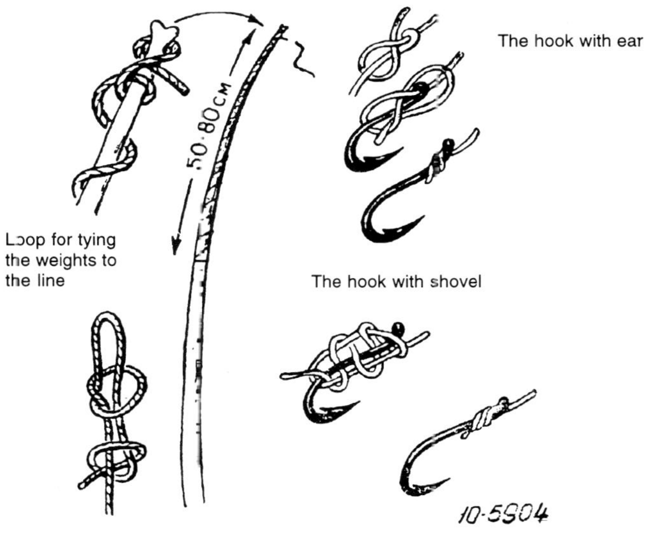

Picture 29. HOW TO TIE FISHING TACKLE

EDIBLE PLANTS

There are a lot of edible plants in the mountains, deserts, tundra.

Flowers, blooms, nuts, onions, suckers, sprouts of a large amount of plants are edible.

Some of them are good to eat raw, such as berries, blooms, others are better to fry or to boil, such as sprouts, and onions.

DON'T EAT:

- Stones and seeds
- Onions, which do not have the characteristic smell which is usual for garlic or onion.
- Plants which have a milk- not a clear colorful juice.
- Mushrooms which have an unpleasant smell.

You can discover if a plant can be eaten by finding out if it is eaten by birds and other animals. Don't eat large amounts if you aren't sure. Try only a small amount (3-5 grams). This amount can not be dangerous even if this plant is poisonous. After tasting, wait 4-5 hours. If during this time you do not suffer nausea, stomachache, headache, diarrhea or constipation- it means that this plant is good for food.

HOW TO COOK

Try to cook warm food at least one time per day, even if you are in very poor condition. Use for that metal cans, the NAZ box from the first-aid kit and other handy supplies.

You can fry onions, suckers, fish and small animals directly on coals, rolling them in the loam. Small animals and birds you can roast on a spit without taking off the fur and feathers. Remove it after roasting, it'll be easier for you.

The method of cooking food under a campfire is very easy. Dig a hole into the ground with a depth of 30-40 cm. Line all of the walls with wet fabric, or live grass. Then put into the hole food and cover with sand to 15-20 cm. Place the fire above it and keep it going until the meal is ready to use.

You can roast the meal on hot stones, covering it with leaves, grass, and then with a cover of sand. Determine the time the food is ready by smell and taste.

Roast or boil the food which remains after yesterday's dinner again. Scrap the fungus away if the meat is covered with it, wash it thoroughly and cook, again.

You can prepare a good meal supply in advance, drying it in the sun or dry curing by slim slices over a fire.

LOCATING WATER SUPPLY

WATER IN THE TAIGA IS NOT DIFFICULT TO LOCATE - If you don't find any natural springs, look for water in narrow gullies, between hills, in dry rivers and creek beds. Sometimes you can find the water at a depth of 1.5 meters. Don't use this kind of water directly, boil it first. You can use as good water the sap of the maple and birch. For this, make vertical or parallel cuts on the bark of the tree. (depth of cut 3-4 cm.) Install a gutter under every cut. Collect the sap in a clean can or cap. You can acquire 1 liter of sap per night.

WATER IN THE ARCTIC - It is easy to fill your water supply in the warm season. The water from lakes, rivers, creeks, is good to drink. But the water of stagnant locations must be boiled.

It is possible to get the water from snow holes, when the snow is melting.

You can collect water from old ice in cold weather. New sea ice is not usable for it has 15% salt. The old ice usually is easy to see by the blue color, new ice is green.

If you can't obtain water, and fire is limited because of limited fuel, it is recommended you fill your water container with snow or ice and melt it under your clothes. Don't drink by eating snow! The amount of water is not great and you may injure your mouth.

WATER IN THE DESERT- the most important element for preserving life. Look for water always in the lowest place: between hills, or in dry river beds. You can often find water at a depth of 1.5-2 meters in these places. Signs to locate water: gnats crowding in a spot in the summer, green plants in the empty desert. In the deserts of Central Asia, the poplar tree can be a good sign of underground water.

TRAVEL ON FOOT

The decision to stay in on location or to leave is the most responsible part of survival. Carefully appraise your situation whether to leave: your health, your strength, your supplies. Think what to take on your hike. First of all, your supplies, your water, food, signal devices, medical kit, boat, etc.

Make a knapsack from the top of your parachute and parachute harness (Picture 30). Don't throw away any parachute parts. They can be useful for shoes or clothing repairs (Picture 31).

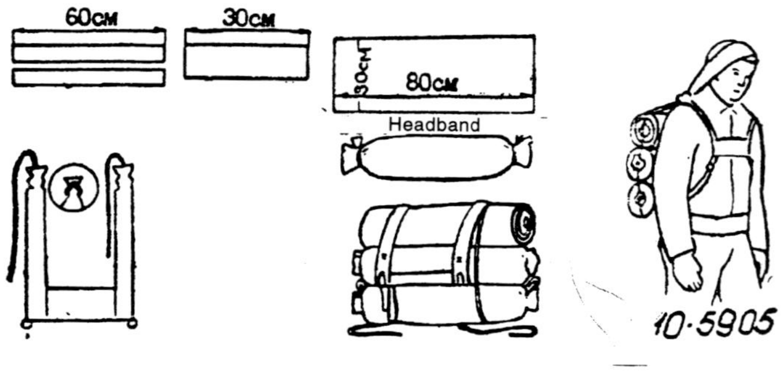

Picture 30. HOW TO CONSTRUCT A KNAPSACK USING PARACHUTE HARNESS AND OTHER PARTS FROM YOUR PARACHUTE AND SURVIVAL KIT START BY CUTTING PARTS OF YOUR PARACHUTE INTO STRIPS IN LENGTHS SHOWN. ALSO MODIFY YOUR PARACHUTE HARNESS INTO A RUCKSACK AS SHOWN ABOVE. CONNECTING SEVERAL BUNDLES TOGETHER ALLOWS MANY ITEMS TO BE CARRIED IN A SECURE MANNER.

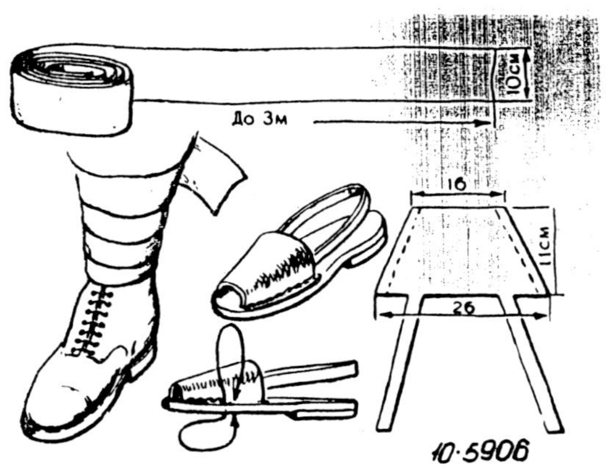

Picture 31. HOW TO CONSTRUCT SHOES AND PUTTEES FROM PARACHUTE MATERIALS CUT PARACHUTE FABRIC INTO STRIPS 2-3m AND 10cm WIDE FOR PUTTEES. SHOES CAN BE CONSTRUCTED BY FOLLOWING THE ABOVE INSTRUCTIONS.

Leave behind in your camp information about your travel direction and your reasons for leaving. Make signs in the forest as cuts in trees leave small pieces of parachute fabric on branches. You will be able to easily find your way back using these signs if it becomes necessary, and it will make it easier for rescue crews to locate you if they locate your camp after you've left.

Try to choose the easiest way through soft, swampy areas, don't walk straight. Rather, take a course which may be much longer but much easier. Step on roots and other solid places. It'll help you preserve your strength.

Assist yourself, walking or swimming through water obstacles with the help of parachute shrouds. Even if the depth of the river or creek is not great, proceed with the help of a walking stick.

Allow for plenty of rest time during your hike. Rest 10-20 minutes for every 1-2 hours you walk. Take at least one long rest for cooking lunch or dinner.

Stop your hike before dark taking into account the time for gathering a supply of combustibles and building a campfire.

HIKING IN THE TAIGA

Use animal trails, tops of hills, and dry rivers. Leave a sign every 150-200 meters to avoid getting lost.

Do not attempt to travel in the taiga in fog without a compass. Avoid all bogs and marshes. Use a long wood pole, if you can't avoid going through. Handle the walking stick at an angle. If you fall into a bog, don't panic and flail around. Save your energy. Don't try to keep your body vertical, it's better to try and crawl your way out using your walking stick for help.

It is very hard and sometimes even impossible to walk without snowshoes in the taiga during winter with its deep snow cover. You can also use snowshoes during travel through the bogs or swamps.

You can make snowshoes as illustrated in picture 32.

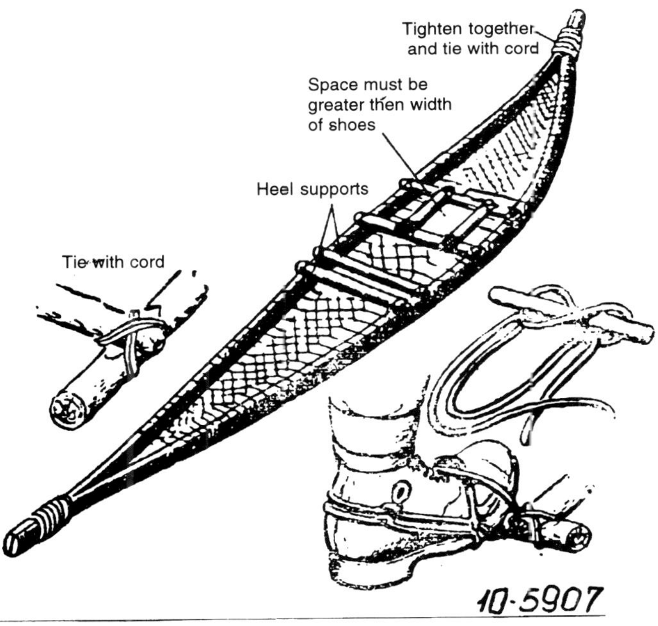

Picture 32. HOW TO CONSTRUCT, WEAR, AND USE SNOWSHOES MADE FROM PARACHUTE AND NATURAL MATERIALS. OBTAIN TWO STRONG LIVE BRANCHES 150cm IN LENGTH AND 2-2.5cm IN DIAMETER. TIE THEM TOGETHER AND 30cm APART IN THE CENTER USING PARACHUTE CORD. USE MORE CORD TO CONSTRUCT THE LACING AS SHOWN ABOVE. ADDITIONAL LACING CAN BE USED TO ATTACH THE SNOWSHOES TO YOUR BOOTS.

In the winter season you can use snowshoes for traveling across frozen rivers.

Remember that the river's current can break lower parts of the ice. The thinnest ice is near sharp, steep banks and under snowhills. Sometimes the level of water in the river can drop and under the ice can be air pockets. This is very dangerous for hiking. If you don't have another way and the ice seems too thin, you should crawl on the ice, pushing the rubber raft ahead of yourself.

While hiking on the river is easier, do not do so any more than necessary. This will make your journey safer. If you are traveling in the raft be careful to avoid any large branches and trees because they can cut or puncture your raft. It is safer to use the raft only on open water. A raft can be constructed with the help of 4-5 tree's trunks (usually pine-trees) with a length of 3-3.5m. and a diameter of 20-30cm. Tie the trunks by curving trees branches or parachute shroud as shown.

It is better to build the raft near the water, so you will not waste energy on transporting it to the river.

Prepare in advance a few strong poles before casting off. Prepare also a fireplace on the raft, covering this area with sand and making a tent upon it. Don't forget to make an anchor. You can do this with the help of a long shroud line with a heavy stone tied on the end.

To secure to the bank: Tie the heavy stone (500-600 grams) to the shroud line. Throw it on the bank and then tie the line to it. If you use a tree, make sure it is reliable, that it is strong and that the river current will not take the raft away. You can see how to make a raft with help of handy materials on picture 33.

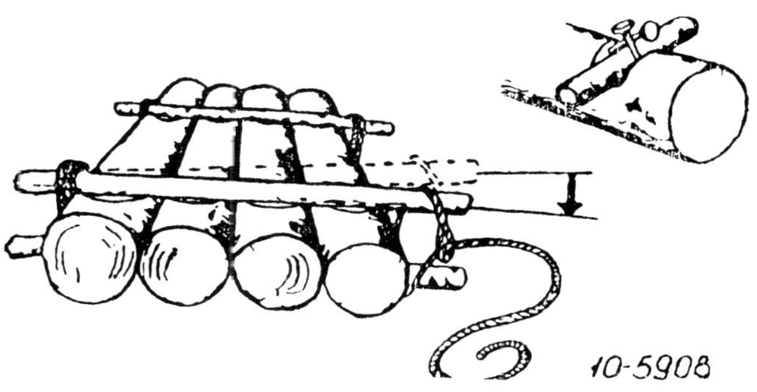

Picture 33. CONSTRUCTING A RAFT USING AVAILABLE MATERIALS

HIKING IN THE ARCTIC

If you have landed on drift-ice, stay in the same location, don't move before help comes. You should leave the landing point only if: you saw an island while you were in the air in your parachute; if the drift-ice is a danger to your life.

Pack all necessary supplies and prepare good shoes before leaving. Make from parachute fabric covers for your feet and put it upon your shoes. Cover your head, neck, and face with the help of a scarf or parachute fabric.

It is very important to orient yourself in the Arctic, because there are not any good natural reference points. It is easy to make a mistake, when you try to determine a distance from one place to another (visually) and also there are a lot of optical illusions (mirage) in the Arctic.

You can't always trust a compass in Arctic conditions. Therefore make a few readings with your compass and count the middle one and use it.

You can determine your coordinates with the help of snow hills. The narrower part of a snow hill will be on the wind side and usually snow hills sharply become higher from underside. Remember, that in some areas in the Arctic, winds can have the same non-changing direction. So the sharp topside of snow hills will show you on the west, in the area's Arctic islands east winds are usual. There are a lot of south winds. So in these areas the sharpest part of the hill will show you which way is north.

You can orient yourself in the Arctic by looking at the sky, unless it is foggy weather. Any other kind of orientation is very difficult. Look carefully at the sky's color. The sky with many clouds can be like a mirror where the ocean surface is reflected. Therefore the clouds that have width shine-upon the icy places, and a dark line on the clouds- will be line of water between ice or cracking in ice surface. Upon large open water there is usually a cloudy, black fog.

Remember that ice with a depth of 10-15cm. may take the weight of a human, but safe depth is 25cm. Assist each other by using a shroudline during travel on ice. It is useful to poke the ice ahead yourself in places where you're not sure. If the ice is very thin, and you can't go any other way- better crawl. Leave your NAZ survival kit on the thick ice, and tie to it the end of a parachute shroud line and tie the other to your left hand. Don't make any quick movements, just crawl very carefully. Push the rubber raft ahead of you. Take off your knife and place it in your right hand.

If you fall through the ice, don't waste any time, swim to a side where you can crawl out. Plunge your knife into the ice and climb out. Then take off your clothes and dry them. If you can't build a fire to assist the drying, cover yourself with a parachute and hang the clothes on any support. Never put yourself and your comrades in risk. Never travel in a snowstorm. Make a temporary dwelling and stay there even if the storm lasts several days.

Travel across the tundra is very difficult because there isn't any natural cover, shelters, or hollows. Winds in the tundra can be very strong, so strong that it can make proceeding impossible. And also there are not enough natural landmarks for orientation and it is therefore hard to find directions or to determine a location. Don't follow the rivers in the tundra, because they are very curvy and windy.

During the summer, rain and fog are common with thaws in the daytime and light frost at night. This makes travel even more difficult in the tundra. Therefore, despite the time of year, make your decision to leave camp or landing location only if you know for certain a settlement is nearby and that you are able to achieve the distance.

HIKING IN THE DESERT

If you decide to leave your landing location prepare and protect your body from the sun's rays and the desert's dryness.

Bandage your legs with parachute fabric; it will decrease abrasion from sand.

Protect your head, neck, face with the help of cover, as shown in picture 34. Pack carefully all your water supplies.

REMEMBER! WITHOUT ENOUGH WATER, HIKING IN THE DAYTIME IS EXTREMELY DANGEROUS. HIKE ONLY IN THE EARLY MORNING OR IN THE EVENING WHEN IT IS NOT AS HOT, OR THROUGHOUT THE WHITE NIGHTS.

Never travel beyond your limit; becoming too tired. Try to rest at the same intervals of time (every 2-3 hours). Choose the easiest way. Protect your feet from blisters. Clean the sand from your shoes and socks regularly. Be ready to signal quickly in case help appears.

Remember that in deserts mirages are often "seen." Don't change your direction even if you see an "oasis", "mountains", "a lake with islands." Or anything else. Make sure it is not a mirage.

Stop hiking in case of a sandstorm. Usually the first signs of a storm are the absence of wind and the sultriness lessens. Hide behind any shelter on the down wind side. Cover yourself with your parachute, and protect your nose and mouth. Bury all water supplies in the ground. A dark cloud on the horizon is usually the sign of a sandstorm. It can last from a few hours to 2-3 days.

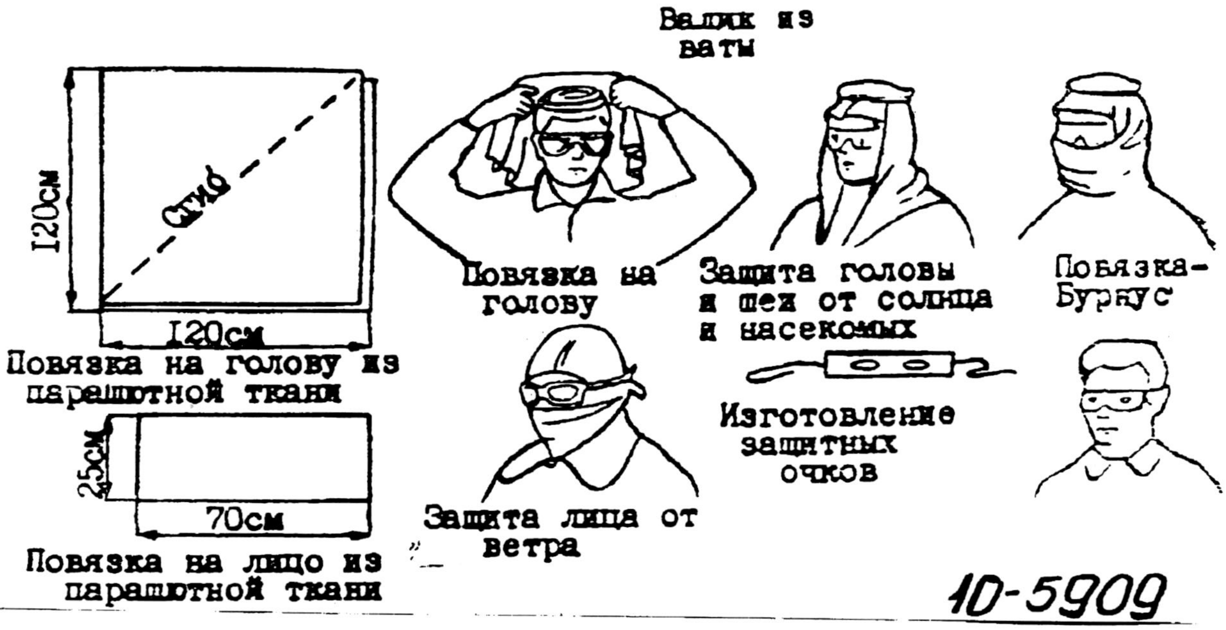

Picture 34. HOW TO CONSTRUCT USEFUL EQUIPMENT TO PROTECT YOURSELF IN THE DESERT FROM THE POWERFUL RAYS OF THE SUN AND FROM THE HEAT BY USING AVAILABLE MATERIALS. HEAD PROTECTION CAN BE CONSTRUCTED FROM PARACHUTE FABRIC. CUT A LENGTH OF 15-20cm AND KEEP IT HANDY TO USE AS COVER FOR YOUR NOSE AND MOUTH IN A SANDSTORM. FOLLOW INSTRUCTIONS ABOVE ON HOW TO WEAR.

INSTRUCTIONS FOR SEA SURVIVAL

After the plane lands, first of all throw out on the water the emergency rubber raft and tie it to the plane. Keep the raft tied until the time when all of the crew members have entered the raft. Put into the raft all water and food supplies. Then cut the line, or rope and paddle away from the plane.

Check the raft for any holes. Check your comrades' conditions and help them as you can. If anyone suffers from sea sickness, give them pills from the first-aid kit in the NAZ survival kit.

Remember that your life directly depends on the raft's condition. Keep away any sharp metal containers, don't leave them without covers because they can damage the raft's surface. Cover the raft with a piece of parachute fabric after the anchor is thrown on the bank, it'll further protect your boat from damage.

During the voyage, check the joints and valves regularly. Check also the raft's inner tubes, they should be smooth and curvy.

During the hot part of the day remove a little bit of air from the inner tubes. In the cold weather, increase the amount.

Fatigue and the lack of food can often be the reason for stress, and nervous shock. The best way to avoid it: full-time activity and timely actions. Try to involve every member of your crew in some type of duty. Organize a watch which will observe surroundings in case of the sudden appearance of land, planes, ships, or boats. Change the watch every 2 hours.

INSTRUCTIONS FOR USING EMERGENCY ISSUE SIGNALLING EQUIPMENT

After you are safely in the raft, ready all the signal supplies. Protect them from water, but always keep them handy.

Use the dye pack with colored powder only in case of observing the plane. For that, open the pack, tie it to the raft, and throw it into the water. Within an instant, it will make a colorful, fluorescent stain, which will be easily seen from a plane.

Always hold the signal cartridge (FSND) in your hand away from your face and body as far as possible. Be careful because the smoke can hit you. Operate it from the down wind side. In sunny weather use the signal mirror. At night, signal with the flare end of the PSND.

You can increase the speed of the raft or reduce it with the help of an anchor and sail.

FOOD AND WATER SUPPLY

Inventory all supplies of food and water. Use the fresh water only for drinking. If you don't have enough water, limit its usage to 500-600 gr. per person, per day. Drink it in small amounts. Cover the water bottle with fabric and regularly wet it by putting it outside the boat in water. It will make the water inside cooler.

You can obtain additional water to drink with the help of the chemical treatment which makes salt water fresh. Look for the packets in your survival kit. They can each supply 1500-3500g of fresh water.

The meat of fish can be a good supply of fresh water. For that, cut the fish meat in pieces, put it in fabric and squeeze it. Put the juice in your water bottle. You can also fill your reserve of water by natural sources: rain, snow, ice, dew.

Never drink sea water, even if you have no other water.

Be thrifty with your food supply.

Fishing- is the best method to get food.

You can use as leader bait small fishes. If you can't catch them, use buttons, small foil pieces, leather, or fabric.

Never eat the eggs or liver from fish.

To prepare the fish meat in advance you can wash, clean, and wash it again out of the raft in water. This makes it slightly salty, cut it into slim pieces and dry/cure it in the sun.

You can use a few kinds of sea weed as food. You can see these types in picture 35.

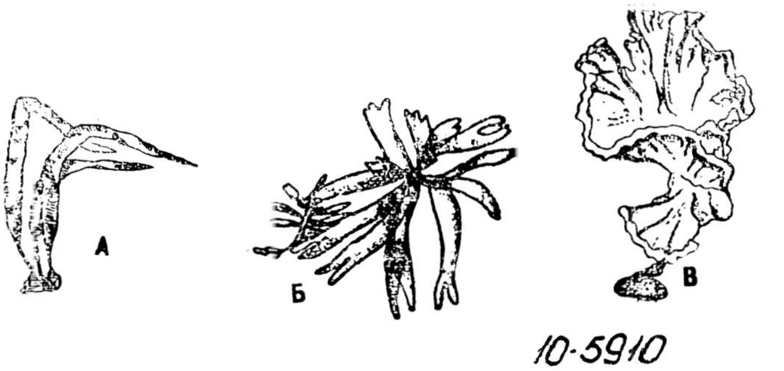

Picture 35. EDIBLE TYPES OF SEAWEED

Disease Treatment

In the tropical water areas the greatest danger is dehydration and the effects of the sun.

Remember, that in hot conditions, the body loses a lot of water from sweat very quickly. To reduce this water loss from your body, use parachute fabric as a cover and stay under it in the sun. Don't do any work during the hotter part of day. Don't remove any clothing, it will help protect you from sunburn. Soak clothes in the water outside the boat. But dry it before dark.

To protect your eyes from the irritation of the sun's reflections, put on sunglasses or if you don't have any, place dark fabric with small slots over your eyes. If you suffer from sea sickness take one or two pills from the first-aid kit, curtail any activity and lay in the bottom of the raft. Temporarily don't eat any food or drink any water.

In the north, the most important consideration is freezing weather. Protect your body from freezing. If you get cold, warm yourself by brisk movements and cover yourself with as much extra clothes and fabric as possible.

As a result of constant water on the skin, it can become dry and irritated. The rash and small cuts are not dangerous, but they are very unpleasant. Carefully bandage the cuts and apply burn ointment on the rash.

Never touch sea snakes; their poison can be dangerous. If you come into contact with one, immediately wash the area and apply sintomicin ointment.

How To Handle Sharks

There are a lot of different kinds of sharks in the tropical oceans and seas, some of them (blue, white, tiger, hammerhead, sand, seafox, brown) can attack people.

Staying in the raft is the safest bet. Don't swim in the open water even if it is very hot. Swimming is permitted only near the banks. But sometimes sharks can swim very close to your raft and even punch it. Don't panic. Don't take any irrational action. You can drive the shark away by knocking your oar in the water.

After your landing on the sea, when you are still in the water, remember these rules:

- Don't take off all of your clothes and shoes.
- Hurry: climb into the raft
- If the raft is nearby, swim to it with careful, strong, rhythmic movements, don't make any unnecessary movements of arms and legs.

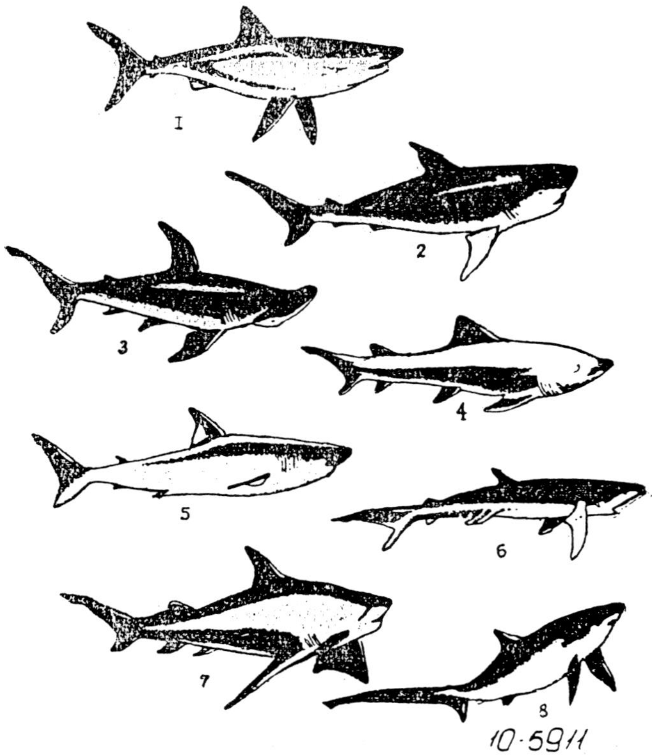

Picture 36. SHARKS WHICH ARE DANGEROUS TO MAN: 1.MAKO; 2.TIGER; 3.HAMMERHEAD SHARK; 4.BROWN; 5.SAND; 6.BLUE; 7.WHITE; 8.SEA FOX

In the boat:

- Don't put your extremities into the water
- Don't throw away any remnants of food or trash
- Remember, Stop fishing if sharks are nearby

Debarkation

If you are on the sea or ocean, try to locate land. There are signs that can be seen that land is nearby:

- If you can see a stationary cloud upon the horizon
- If you can see pieces of trees, branches, leaves, grass
- Changing of water color, from dark to light.

Usually you can find land if you see birds flying in the evening. The direction in which they fly will be towards land.

With the decision to reach land by swimming, put on your life preserver. Watch for sharp stones and rocks, as they can easily injure you or damage your raft.

If you debark on the bank with dense bush, stay on the narrow land near the water. Don't venture in land until you can see there are no bogs or sharp rocks.

AIRCREW PROCEDURES IN A RADIOACTIVE ENVIRONMENT

If you have landed in an area that is radioactive, your first actions must be to protect yourself from contamination.

Consider the level of contamination the area might have been be exposed. Radioactivity can be caused by gamma, beta, and alpha emissions. The most dangerous is gamma emissions. It can cause severe illness, if you get 50R. Sometimes you can feel only the first reaction- nausea, headache, and weakness. It can take from a few minutes to four hours. After that the symptoms will disappear, and you will feel as well as before. This should be reported to your doctor, later.

Beta-emissions cause radioactive burns on the skin and eye surfaces. Alpha-emissions can be dangerous only if you have consumed contaminated food or water.

Determine the radiation level, if you have a gygercounter. Try to leave the area if it is more than 50R/hour. Travel quickly and perpendicularly to the wind direction. If the level is more than 50R/hour, immediately take cover in any dwelling, trench, or cavern.

If the location has no protection, quickly clean off an area, removing 1-2 cm. of dirt with your snowshoe or knife. Then lay in it and make a deeper trench as you can.

Shake the parachute fabric well and cover yourself with it.

Tuck it around you. Even the thin material will help protect you from the radiation. To reduce by half the gamma radiation, use a wall of stones with thinness of 9.5cm., or ground- 13cm., or wood-25cm., or snow-30cm.

Remember, that with time the radioactive level is reduced. In 7 hours, the level is only 1/10, in 49 hours- 1/100, in 2 weeks-1/1000: But this level is renewed following each new detonation. If you can not determine the level of radioactivity, stay in the shelter at least 24 hours.

Food and Water

Use your NAZ survival kit food first in a radioactive environment because the containers offer good protection.

But re-stock your supply by hunting, fishing, and useful plants, if it is possible.

You should very carefully process any animal meat.

Do not eat the heart, liver, or any meat which is touching bones.

Wash thoroughly the vegatables and fruits, because it will reduce the radiation by 80-90%

The water in rivers can be radioactive. To avoid it, dig a hole 30-40cm. from river with a depth of 40-50cm. The water which will seep in, even if it is not very clean, will be safe after boiling. You can also put in the water one pill of pantocid.

Water of creeks can be used fresh.

Clothing

Don't remove your gloves and hat. You can decrease the level of exposure on your clothing by shaking them well and rinsing in running water. Wash the dust from open body parts. In case of a burn, wash the area quickly with water from your NAZ kit and then bandage.

JET AGE FLIGHT HELMETS
Aviation Headgear in the Modern Age

Alan R. Wise & Michael S. Breuninger

This new photo documentation is the first book ever to cover in detail the history and development of military flight helmets from the post-World War II era to the present, and includes over 120 different helmets and their associated equipment such as oxygen masks, boom microphones, inner helmets etc. U.S. Air Force, Army, Navy, Marine Corps, and Coast Guard flight helmets discussed range from standard fighter, bomber, transport and helicopter models, to high-altitude, special purpose and experimental types. Foreign helmets covered include British, French, German Swedish, Canadian, and rarely documented Polish, Chinese and Soviet/Russian models. Also covered is an extensive selection of U.S. and Soviet/Russian space helmets. Extensively researched this book contains over 1000 images, most in color, and includes multiple-view photographs as well as detail views. Specific details of each helmet include manufacturer, proper designation, unique features, accessories, periods of use, branch of service(s), and aircraft in which it was used – selected export users are also included.

Size: 9" x 12" over 1000 color and b/w photographs
248 pages, hard cover
ISBN: 0-7643-0070-9 $75.00

UNITED STATES COMBAT AIRCREW SURVIVAL EQUIPMENT
World War II to the Present - A Reference Guide for Collectors

Michael S. Breuninger

This book is a detailed study of United States Air Force, Army, Army Air Force, Navy, and Marine Corps aircrew survival equipment. Among the items covered are: survival vests, leggings and chaps, life preservers, survival (ejection) seat and back pad kits, personal survival kits and first aid kits, and various survival components. Tag and label information is provided for each item.

Size: 8 1/2" x 11" over 170 b/w photographs, drawings
208 pages, soft cover
ISBN: 0-88740-791-9 $29.95

Also from the publisher